Hedge Witch

Rae Beth has been studying Pagan traditions and women's mysteries for many years. Her interest grew when her involvement with the women's movement and her work as an astrologer and tarot consultant converged in Goddess spirituality. She became a self-initiated witch in 1978, perceiving the role of witch as a poetic symbol of women's psychic strength, as well as a key to the resurgence of Pagan ideals, such as a reverence for the Earth. Later, she also came to understand the role of the male witch, as present-day shaman and brother to the wisewoman or witch priestess.

Born a schoolteacher's daughter, she was once a student teacher herself, specializing in English literature. She now writes magical poetry. An active environmentalist, Rae Beth lives just outside Bath, where she enjoys country walks, and is married with two children.

Hedge Witch

A Guide to Solitary Witchcraft

RAE BETH

ROBERT HALE · LONDON

© Rae Beth 1990
First published in Great Britain 1990
First paperback edition 1992
Reprinted 1994 (twice)
Reprinted 1995
Reprinted 1996

Robert Hale Limited
Clerkenwell House
Clerkenwell Green
London EC1R 0HT

ISBN 0-7090-4851-3

8 10 12 14 15 13 11 9

Photoset in Garamond by
Derek Doyle & Associates, Mold, Clwyd.
Printed in Great Britain by
St Edmundsbury Press Limited, Bury St Edmunds, Suffolk.
Bound by WBC Bookbinders Limited.

All line illustrations drawn by Bill Wright

Introduction

The following letters were not meant to be in a book, originally. They were written as lessons for two apprentice witches. For the real-life Tessa and Glyn. Then I realized that this could well be a book of interest to many who are seeking a path of nature magic, but who are unprepared, for one reason or another, to involve themselves with covens.

Tessa and Glyn have been taught in an old tradition, that of the solitary or 'hedge' witch. This is rather like the old-time village wisewoman or wiseman: one who 'knows' and worships the Goddess and her consort, the Horned God; one who practises spellcraft for the purposes of healing, and teaches the mysteries. Though this is sometimes a lonely path, it leads to places of great beauty. Parts of it can be walked in company with others, but the magical workings are always done alone, or with one magical partner. This suits some of us, for there is a certain kind of witch at home with solitude. He or she need not be friendless. But by temperament, some are drawn to worship and work magic on their own, and to fulfil a different archetype from that of coven member. To them, and to my husband and magical partner Cole Campion, this book is dedicated.

Rae Beth
Yule 1988
The West of England

Part One

New Green
Avonford

8th January 1987

Dear Tessa and Glyn,
I will answer your question, 'What is witchcraft?' in letter form. And I will start with the most surprising things I can think of. The biggest surprise to most people about witches, once they have realized we are not 'devil-worshippers' nor 'tools of the powers of evil' (in true horror-movie style), is that we worship a female deity, a Goddess. We also worship a God. That does not really surprise anyone. But reverence for the Mother of All Life, in this culture, is unexpected. It has implications, spiritually, emotionally and socially.

Historically, witches have been persecuted for their belief in a Goddess. It was politically unacceptable in a patriarchal culture. Worship of a Goddess would have to mean, for example, that the earth, Mother Earth, would once again be held sacred. She could no longer be polluted or exploited for any reason, and a great deal of power and profit would be lost by unscrupulous men. Better, from their point of view, to worship a God who is all mind and spirit, 'out there' up in heaven, away from the disgusting, 'sinful' Earth.

In the spiritual view of our modern world, femaleness has long been reckoned as not quite so holy as maleness. Woman, in all the world's patriarchal religions – Christianity and Islam in particular – is seen as the bringer of sin, a snare and a trap for the 'holier' sex. Closer to animality, through menstruation and childbirth, and to the earth. How can there be a God who is female? most people would now ask. Witches would answer that childbearing *is* the original creative act, and that prehistoric people worshipped both gods and goddesses (primarily goddesses) since time out of mind. This is shown by the earliest mythologies, and by the numerous pictures and statues of goddesses which have been found at ancient sites all over the world.

Nowadays, some witches, in rebellion against the cruel

11

suppression of Goddess worship, would actually go so far as to say that only the Goddess should be worshipped. An understandable but sad reaction. However, the Father of All Life, the God, must be acknowledged too. He exists and his suppression would be as destructive as the suppression of all knowledge of the Mother Goddess. The true aim of witchcraft is reconciliation of opposites. Bitterness, hatred and resentment between the sexes is as old as history, but witchcraft is the only religion which has as its avowed aim the healing of these wounds. Sadly, there are those in the world, of both sexes, who have no desire for reconciliation or perhaps no belief that such a thing is possible. To them, for them, I cannot speak. But I can speak to you two and perhaps to others. What I am saying is that witchcraft, at least potentially, is a religion of healing.

Where does it gain its credentials? What is its history? Witchcraft is Paganism. More specifically, it is a type of Paganism with roots in our neolithic past. It has evolved and endured through thousands of years of persecution. In the present day, it is a system of beliefs and magical practices dedicated to restoring the lost harmony between humanity and the subtle, transrational aspects of life, the mysteries. Our belief is that this would restore, also, the lost harmony between humanity and Mother Earth. Though it is now new, reborn, it was, in fact, a form of the Old Religion. Perhaps, now, you can see why it has been dubbed as evil. For such slander is the standard practice of an incoming religion displacing an old one. Witches, then, are not necessarily evil. They are simply followers of a religion which predated Christianity.

Second surprising fact: witches are not always elderly women, although they can be. In any case, they are no more prone to warts than the average member of the population (though considerably better at charming warts away). They are not recognizable. Not only do they not wear tall black hats, but they could be of any age and either sex. (The men are called witches, too; not warlocks, as some people think.) Some work in covens, some alone and some, like myself, with

12

one magical partner. But you have no way of knowing who among your neighbours might be one. It could be anybody.

Yes, they do practise magic. Not to curse or to undermine but to help and heal. Does it work? Does magic achieve anything? Third surprising fact: yes. But it has to be learned, like anything else.

Also, yes, witches do sometimes work naked in their rites. Even solitary witches do this, for we believe in the sacredness of all our bodies and we enjoy the freedom and beauty of going 'skyclad'. Furthermore, tradition says that magic can be worked more effectively like this, as clothes can impede the flow of the witch's etheric energy. It is for warm weather, of course, or by a blazing fire. There is nothing magically effective about gooseflesh!

Well, I hear you ask next, now you've let on about nakedness, what about Old Nick, with the horns and the forked tail? What about Old Hornie? Don't you really worship the Devil? No smoke without fire.

Old Hornie? Yes. The Devil, principle of evil? No. The Horned God, to witches, is male partner of the Triple Goddess. He is dynamic, the life force, male aspect of all nature. We worship him because we worship life. He has horns and a tail to denote his instinctive and animal knowledge, his nature wisdom. This God is part beast and part man, a blend of the life force and shamanic skills. The Horned God, like the Goddess, is sexual, earthy, passionate and wise. Cruel and evil he is not. Between these two, the Mother Goddess and her partner, the world was made. They made it by desire and by love. Therefore, their sexuality is the sacred life force and it follows that, to witches, our own sexuality is sacred, a true spiritual experience. Potentially, the most spiritual of all experiences.

Perhaps that is the most surprising fact of all about witchcraft. It shouldn't be. But I have to admit that in this world as it actually is most people find it hard to equate sex and spirituality. It goes against everything patriarchal religions have taught about sex being shameful and disgusting – at best, a necessity for the continuation of the species.

13

Are you still with me, still interested? If so, ask more questions. I will do my best to answer everything because I want to set the record straight. I and my fellow witches are tired of being seen as the wearers of tall black hats who make revolting bats' wing soup and hang about in churchyards in the dead of night collecting dead men's fingernails. I don't. We don't.

So if the mention of the Horned God (sex!) hasn't put you off, write back or call round. Ask more questions. I will go on answering in letter form as this gives me the chance to think about what I want to say and then to express myself (I hope) more clearly. I will write the same letter to each of you and send a copy to your separate addresses, while I will keep a copy for my own reference. It is good to have the chance to tell the truth and to be listened to with sympathy. All blessings to you both.

Blessed be,
Rae

New Green
Avonford

16th January 1987

Dear Tessa and Glyn,
So you both want to be witches? It is easy to understand why Tessa feels this way. Witchcraft offers women an opportunity to worship a female deity. It reveals a truth that women have waited too long to see vindicated: that divinity is female, as well as male.

It is less easy to see why men want to become witches, at first sight. But many do. The rewards are as great as for women, in the long run. There is freedom from old conflicts, for example, like that between sensuality and spirituality. The Horned God, the male deity of witches, does not present men with an image of immediate male superiority (or inferiority). Instead, the image is of natural wisdom and wildness. Powerful as a stag is powerful, or a tree; not as a dictator, or a nuclear missile. This demands a sacrifice of old ideas. The Horned God has no automatic upper hand, in worldly terms. But to be at one with the body *and* the spirit is a dream that men have not been able to fulfil for too long.

For both men and women, the experience of celebrating the eight festivals each year, and the Full Moon rites, is a complete joy. There is, too, the promise of a self-determined path, your only guides being life, and the information that it brings you, your own inner wisdom and the Goddess, together with the Horned God. No gurus, no authorities and no dogma.

Whatever your reasons for being interested, it seems you already feel drawn to witchcraft. I am convinced that hedge witchcraft, and all forms of modern Paganism, have an important part to play in this world. But do you know what it will do to your lives? This is not an easy path to tread and to enter upon it is a major undertaking for anyone. The same is true, of course, of any spiritual path. (And I know that most people would look askance at the word 'spiritual' in

15

connection with the word 'witch'.)

If you have been a witch before (and witches do accept the idea of reincarnation), then you will want to come back to it. Indeed, there is an old saying, 'Once a witch, always a witch,' meaning you will be drawn back in life after life. If this idea fills you with panic, better not begin! But if it makes your heart lift, you are in good company. Many men and women have found the true essence of happiness as a witch, a priest or priestess of natural magic. Many have died for their faith, it meant so much to them, in the Burning Times (the great persecution by the Christian Church). Thank the Goddess, we do not face such a terrifying threat now, simply for believing as we do and practising the Craft. But socially, and sometimes in other ways, there can be problems. Centuries of bad propaganda have robbed the image of a female witch of strength and dignity, denying all her true aspirations and her magical, transcendent knowledge, as well as the vital part she once played in the life of her community as healer, midwife and counsellor. She has been reduced to a caricature of evil. The male witch, if admitted to exist at all, is generally thought to be an unusually gross kind of 'black' magician. On being told that a real witch is standing in front of them, many people will assume that you must be a sinister person or you wouldn't be practising such an extraordinary religion. Alternatively, they believe you can't be a 'real' witch, after all, because you are too nice. Be that as it may, a witch has his or her rewards (in *this* life, not only in the next!) because a witch can never be dead to meaning or to true magic.

To be fully alive is worth everything. Such open sensitivity can entail suffering, but joy is real. You know the blessing of the Sun, intensely. Likewise, you feel the cold of winter. You are alive to Moon and Earth and every magical vibration from a stone or flower, candle flame or pool of water. You feel the pain of others, as well as your own, in your heart or in your body. And the Earth's pain, as she is drilled into, sprayed with pesticides, despoiled and stored with nuclear waste. To be a witch can be to tread a line between great joy and great despair or to move back and forth between these two. That is how it is to be completely alive in the world of now. And you will have responsibilities: to celebrate the changing seasons and phases of the Moon; to reconcile the conflicts in yourself, as well as between yourself and others; and to undertake certain rites for all life forms, on their behalf, so that *someone* will greet the newborn Sun, for instance, at the winter solstice – so that *someone* will invoke for fruitfulness and peace throughout the land. You will, along with other witches, eat the Bread of Life at Lammas (Lughnasadh) on behalf of all people. A witch works magically for life, as well as practically. (But a practical deed can carry magical significance.)

Are you ready for all this? Or do you just want to learn a few spells, so that you can get a job, a house or something else you might want? If that is so, I wish you well, and nature magic can assist you certainly. But you cannot call yourself a witch; you will not have become a priest or priestess. You will not have taken on that responsibility or known those particular magical blessings.

We are approaching Imbolg or Candlemas, as the Christians have called their festival, which is held on the same day. (It is a pleasant and evocative name and many witches also use it.) It is the time of the first stirrings of spring, when, in the words of the modern witch, Diana Demdike, '... the Goddess returns to Her people, once more virgin, once more bringing blessings'. And this festival, around 2nd February, used to be the traditional time for the initiation of new witches. Nowadays, any of the eight festivals (Sabbats) can be the right time, or any Full Moon. In the past, though, it was usual to let a whole year go by, during which the neophyte would probably have studied and communed with the great life forces, the principles of changing tides and cycles, and also received training in the basic skills of trancework. This gave time to consider the seriousness of full commitment. The year is said to have run from Imbolg to Imbolg and then initiation was given.

I cannot initiate you. Rather, I will not. I am a hedge witch, a solitary witch. I belong to no coven (although I have known other witches who do and who find that, for them, it is the best way). I cannot teach you about covens either, because I do not belong to one. I work with my magical partner, to whom I am lucky enough to be married. If I had no magical partner, I would always work alone. For me, friendship with other witches is good. We exchange ideas and we support each other. But I work at my own pace and in my own way, with Cole or by myself, because it suits my temperament and circumstances. For if you lack money or have children to consider, or if you have a demanding job (and I know that two of these things apply to each of you), then it is really not feasible to celebrate the Sabbats and Full Moons regularly, at someone else's choice of hour in someone else's house, some distance from your home.

For these and many other reasons, some witches prefer to be a lone priest or priestess of natural magic, open to requests for healing spells or for advice or divination from the people who live near them. Modern wisemen or wisewomen. And so they may take the name 'hedge witch', being outside the mainstream of modern witchcraft, outside all covens. It is, in fact, a different archetype to that of coven witch. Both are witches, but the hedge witch is a solitary being. She or he works alone, from and often for a particular town or village. Such people have always existed.

Nowadays, our function as midwives and healers for the community has been usurped. Nevertheless, it is a rare witch who is not knowledgeable about the emotional and spiritual implications of a birth for mother, father and small infant. Most also know about dietary requirements and the more subtle foundations of good health – the psychological and psychic factors. Many can offer some kind of health counselling or even therapy. Any witch worth the name will also know when to refer a person to a trained therapist or doctor. But it is magical healing which was and is our particular province.

A word of caution. It is important to know when to say no to any request you may get for magical assistance. Not everyone is best helped by a spell, or even by counselling or divination. You are not there to be a crutch or prop to everyone. Nor could you be, for you are still human. Witches are not magically, or in any other way, omnipotent. (You may be surprised by how much other people both wish and fear that you are, however!)

Have I digressed? No, it is all relevant. You cannot take this step unless you know what it may bring. And it is much easier to start than it may be stop, once you are committed. This is not because anyone will make you do anything. There are no authorities in witchcraft, no 'King Witch' who rules over the whole of witchdom. (From time to time, people have cropped up claiming this title for themselves, but no true witch would give them any credence.) In spirit, witchcraft is non-hierarchical. But *inner* causes, things that you yourself have stimulated, can have long-term effects, even into other lives. 'Once a witch, always a witch.'

Now I will say more about initiation. To a hedge witch, this is one's own responsibility. Indeed, this must always be the case, even if someone else thinks they have initiated you. Such a change must always come down to inner experience and readiness, and is between you and the Goddess and God.

Do you want to go ahead? You, Glyn, were enthusiastic about Imbolg when I talked to you on the phone. You wanted to know more. And I know that you have been working simple spells for some time now. And, Tessa, when I saw you in the street, I felt that you were now fully decided.

Let me know what you think. We will take it further if you wish.

Blessed be,
Rae

New Green
Avonford

27th January 1987

Dear Tessa and Glyn,
  Somehow I find it hard to start these letters. Shall I just plunge straight in, describe Imbolg? First, I must say that I am really glad that you both want to go ahead, that you feel you have found your right path. It is wrong for witches to attempt to convert anybody. That is a rule of our religion. So if you had shown no more interest, you would have heard no more about it.
  I know that you want to know about Imbolg first, Glyn. There is so much else I should say, if this festival is to be clear to you, in its full meaning. But I must start somewhere. I will start here, then. And add in other things as they occur.
  Each of the eight Sabbats in the year celebrates a phase in the relationship between the Goddess and the Horned God, Mother/Father Nature, according to season. Imbolg is about beginnings. I call it Brideday. Bride is one of the Goddess's many names. Though it was Christianized as the feast of St Brigid, the older Pagan festival referred to Bride, the Triple Goddess, in her maiden aspect. It is early spring. She is a young girl; she is at the beginning. Like her, we all (whether men or women) dream and make plans, and are inspired towards our future achievements. The Goddess's three aspects of Maid, Mother and Crone stand for enchantment, ripeness and wisdom, in keeping with the three phases of a woman's life. So at Imbolg, the Goddess will sing to us and through us of new enchantment by poetry and love. In spring, the mind and the body both find new inspiration. Thus, Bride is Goddess of poetry, as well as of fertility (and of healing and smithcraft, traditionally).
  There are other themes being played out at Imbolg. It is a time of cleansing and purification. Spring-cleaning now prepares our minds and bodies for a resurgence. Bride the Maiden sweeps away the debris of winter and last year's

growth with her new broom. Like all young people, she is keen on new ways and new ideas. Like her, we must prepare and clear the ground for something new. It is the time of youthfulness and inspiration.

The young God, the Youth, approaches Bride with desire. He is courting her. As lovers (notice the nearby St Valentine's Day, preserving the old beliefs), they inspire each other in mind and body. Their love finds expression in their sexual union. Through this, there will be future growth and fruitfulness, and new life will come into being. Like the young God, we all bring the spark of energy to our plans now: the upsurge of determination, action, which gives life.

In nature, we see the approach of Bride as Mother Earth puts forward the first spring flowers. We see the God in the young growing light of the sun.

I wrote this rather Elizabethan-sounding poem for the last Bride festival. It gives some idea of the themes of this turning-point.

Resurgence

Spring anew,
flowers grow.
From lovers true,
sweet poems flow.
As light enchants
shall the seed dance.
Now resurge both life and love,
earth young again,
young sun above.

Leafbud and snowdrop, see!
Bird sings from bare, bleak tree.
First signs of what shall be.

Light candles to Bride.
Spring shoot, waken seed.
Inspire, word and deed.
Spring fire,
first stirrings of the light.

The most simple kind of Imbolg celebration can be tranquil, meditative. As a lone witch, you might place fresh spring flowers in your room on 2nd February. In the evening, you might light a candle to the worship of the Maiden and the Young God, and then give thanks for the inspiration of the spring light. Then you might dream and ponder, meditating deep within yourself about old ways and old ideas you now mean to leave behind, with winter. Then turn to the new ideas and plans you hope to see come into being in your future life. Imagine, also, the banishing of world hunger, or industrial pollution, or else threats of nuclear war. See these left behind in a winter phase of the world's life. Then imagine a fresh world of balanced ecology. Humankind and the whole Earth in harmony, a world of peace, happiness and plenty.

Light a candle for three dreams or wishes and place these around the room. Light each from the main candle, the first one you lit. This is the Festival of the First Stirrings of the Light, in keeping with the spring. You have just performed a simple spell.

Tradition states that it is not worth trying to cast more than three spells on any one occasion. Magical concentration cannot be stretched any further than that. It is also traditional that spells for other people should come before any magic you do for yourself. So if you were lighting three candles, then the first might be for the world, the second for a friend, the third for some new project of your own. These rules are there for guidance rather than for strict adherence, but they are worth bearing in mind.

I imagine you are now both thinking, How can magic be so simple? How can something as easy as lighting a candle change anything? The answer? It doesn't. What makes the difference is your thought. Magic is the power of thought. Lighting the candle is a device for focusing your thought. It is also a small offering to the powers of Nature, to whom you attune yourself, in thought. If by thought and imagining (of which more later) you have correctly altered your own state of consciousness you become at one with the beings, the energies, or the life tides and currents you have invoked at the

moment of casting your spell. It is these which then bring the spell to fruition, make it work. If you have inadvertently, or even purposely, spelled for a manipulative, selfish or destructive end, it is unlikely to come to fruition if the deities to whom you are attuned are averse to this sort of behaviour – if they are, in fact, the true Goddess of the Circle of Rebirth and the Horned God. You would be aligning yourself with creativity, in order to work a destructive spell. Something would have to give. So you see it is of the utmost importance in whose names you work your magic. And a simple act like lighting three candles from a fourth one can be charged with magical effectiveness, for good or ill, or else be completely flat. It is you, the witch, who make the difference.

However, most witches will want to work a more complex ritual than that described above. They will want the full magic circle, 'sacred space between the worlds'. I will leave it to the next letter to describe how this is done, that is, how the circle is cast, but the rite will begin with an invocation to the Lady and the Lord. That means that the Goddess will be welcomed first with poetry, song or spoken declaration, in which her presence is requested (not that she is ever absent) and her blessing asked. The God is then invoked in the same way. Thus, consciousness is heightened, and connections made in the inner world.

The invocation can be simple or elaborate. A simple version would be like this:

> *I call upon the Triple Goddess of the Circle of Rebirth, she who brings all life into being. She who shines in the night sky with beauty, and enriches all the Earth with mystery. She who is the wisdom of the stars, the pulse of blood and the slow growth of trees. May her presence guide me and her blessing be upon me, for I am of her creation.*

To request the presence of the Horned God, you might say:

> *Horned one, All Father, by the bone, the antler and claw, by the dark forest, by wildness, fierce joy and passion, by all that is untamed, free, be here as the leap of life, undeniable, that I may serve life, being at one with it.*

Magic may be done in the Lady's name only, if it is a spell for something specially connected with her. Likewise, spells may be cast, though less often, in his name alone. Usually, witches will work in both their names, remembering that deity is male and female, and that the interaction between the two great creative forces is what makes the worlds. In this, witchcraft resembles Taoism, recognizing life as the result of interplay between the male and female forces.

Traditionally, the Goddess is said to be 'first among equals'. This is partly because witchcraft has roots in the earliest forms of Paganism, which were matriarchal. Also, scientists have now discovered that femaleness seems, in evolutionary terms, to have come first. Maleness was born from it, apparently as a means of strengthening the species through the diversity of chromosome combinations possible in sexual reproduction. The sex which gives birth came first, while that which impregnates appeared later on. This may be another reason for the Goddess's paradoxical elevation above, yet equality with, the God.

To continue with your Sabbat celebration, you might next stand facing the altar, and read or say aloud:

> *This is the Festival of Bride. I welcome the Triple Goddess, I celebrate and I acknowledge her as Maid. For this is the First Stirrings of the Light, the dawn of spring. The Goddess is again young. She banishes all that is outworn. She sweeps clean on Earth. And with the Young God of the Growing Light, new Lord of Day, she now prepares us for ecstasy, for love, for inspiration. In her name, I clear the ground, I clean and sweep and I prepare a place.*

The lone witch will then ritually sweep the floor within the magical circle with a besom, traditional witch's broom made from birch, sweeping away all the outworn, symbolically. (To spring-clean the house in the period just before Imbolg is also a ritual act. Old, unwanted books, clothes or ornaments may be thrown out, along with their associations, or sold or given away. This makes a space for the new.)

The circle should be swept anticlockwise, widdershins, for this is the banishing direction. Think about what you are magically sweeping away, from the world and also from your own life. What needs to go for new creative possibilities to be realized? Despair? Lack of insight? Fear? Limitations imposed by hierarchy? Refusal to change? Guilt? Alienation? Loneliness? Deprivation? Choose that which you feel most strongly about, and visualize it being swept up. Throw straws or paper scraps in front of your broom to represent the several aspects of this thing, naming them as you do so. When the scraps are all in one heap, place them in a box or tin at the south point of your circle. Later, when you have finished the ritual, burn them.

Put down the broom and dance clockwise, Sunwise, in a

25

newly freshened circle of the world, and of your life, to welcome spring – its inspiration, its resurgence.

Sing, *Spring fire! first stirrings of the light* as a magical chant while you dance round and round the circle. Picture the effect on earth, on nature, of the lengthening of days. See snowdrops, the first leafbuds. See the lightening in the air, the first signs of spring. (When snow is on the ground, this is more a matter of faith! And yet there is something perceptible, for this is a turning-point. Allow yourself to feel it.)

When you finish dancing, place your hands around the base of an unlit candle, in consecration. This small candle will now be sacred to the light of inspiration. Light it, saying, *Burn brightly, for you are of the sun. I dedicate you to inspiration, by the Maiden Goddess and the new Lord of Day.*

Now, small candles are lit from the big, main candle, each one for some new seed idea or dream, an invocation to make it grow with spring light and be brought to fruition. Arrange the candles in a ring around the main candle. Not everyone has enough small candles to do this, but birthday-cake candles will do, in a circle of Plasticine. I suppose this would shock practitioners of High Magic, for there is nothing ceremonial here! But I am of the opinion that the Goddess especially inclines to Kitchen Magic, for things like birthday-cake candles and holders are available to anyone. They are unpretentious. The visual effect is good and, magically, I can vouch for the fact that they do work. Actually, I believe this kind of thing is the essence of hedge witchcraft, if not of all witchcraft. You need to make the 'Crown of Lights' for Bride, so you look around the house and find your kid's Plasticine and left-over candles from his or her last birthday, plus some unused holders. This is magic in the midst of life. And though it would be lovely to buy, if you could afford it, brand new beeswax candles and three pottery holders, it would be no more effective magically.

Light each candle with some words of invocation. *I light this candle to —— [here name your chosen plan or wish].* A lone witch will have a maximum of three small candles around the large one (for maximum concentration, just the three spells or wishes). A couple will have three candles each.

Your invocations must be for the good of those around you, and for life in general, whether they are invocations for your own needs to be fulfilled, or for someone else's. That is, they must be harmonious. They must also be in your own best interests. Witches have only one commandment, called the Witches' Rede, but it is unequivocal: 'Harm none.' I do not believe that either of you would intentionally use magic to attempt to control or manipulate another person's life. But mistakes can be made, inadvertently, for we mortals cannot always know the best solution to any situation. And there is another belief: 'What you send returns to you, threefold, whether for good or ill.'

Invocations for peace of mind or peace on earth or healing, or for the right (unnamed) lover to come to you, or for yourself or another to be rid of addiction to tobacco (or whatever) are obviously not harmful. But no spell should ever be cast without deep consideration of all the implications of its successful outcome. It is never right to interfere with another person's autonomy, and some would go so far as to say that even a healing spell should not be cast without the permission of the person for whom it is being done. It is not, actually, a bad idea to be that cautious, for magic is rarely ineffectual, but sometimes, like anything else, it does backfire.

Above all, remember the life of Mother Earth, for you are a priest or priestess of nature magic. Human needs can and should be met, but not at the expense of the environment, not by ignoring Earth's needs. This would be a betrayal of your true role.

After the candle-lighting, it is good to bring an offering and place it on your altar, to Bride. This should be something you have already felt inspired to do: a piece of pottery, some sewing, a song or poem, a picture, an idea for something connected with your job, some small piece of metalwork, or woodwork, whatever you have. Lay it on the altar, with thanks. It is symbolic of dedicating all future work to the Goddess.

Conclude your ritual with a communion, a joining with the Goddess and the God, by eating bread or cakes and drinking wine which you have lightly covered with your hands and asked them to bless and to make sacred. (If, for any reason, you do not want to drink wine, or if you haven't got any, fruit juice will do. Come to that, water will do, but is best with a dash of wine or some apple concentrate as this is supposed to be a joyful communion, not a prisoner's pittance!)

Any festival of Full Moon rite should end with a communion. This is not a parody of a Christian communion, since it is something far older. It is acknowledgement and celebration of the love between the Goddess and the God who made the world, the bread and wine, and you. It is a way of joining with them, with all life.

I have said much about the Goddess and the God in whose names we work. But who are they? This is a subject for the next letter, since there is much to be said. And it should, perhaps, have been said first. But I knew you would like to know what witches do, at a present-day Sabbat. I have tried to give you some idea, in simple terms, of what a hedge witch does.

Meanwhile, think about the Goddess and the God as archetypal first parents of all life: not making the world in one moment and then standing back, outside creation; but continually involved, involving, manifest, as well as reachable through poetry and myth and inner exploration.

I hope this makes some things clear.

I do not mean either of you to do the full ritual, the one I have just described. That is for next Bride Day. Since I have not yet described the casting of a circle, the instructions are not complete. However, I would like you to do the simple version, if you wish. Light candles, meditate and see how you personally experience this time of year, and what you feel inspired to do.

I will tell how to cast a circle fairly soon, so that you can try a full ritual, if you want to, before initiation. You may wonder why in that case, you need bother with initiation, if you can work magic, worship, do everything in fact, without it. Well, one answer to that is that this is one initiation, now. You will, to a degree, be initiated the minute you first celebrate the turning tides and seasons in any way at all. Full formal self-initiation, in the sense in which we have been discussing it, is the first step on a path of complete commitment. Before that, you can still turn back. By the time that you get close to it, you will know whether you want to.

Blessed be,
Rae

New Green
Avonford

20th February 1987

Dear Tessa and Glyn,
I promised to tell you more about the God and Goddess of
the witches. We have also just celebrated Imbolg (Brideday)
and I should like to put this festival in context, to give a whole
view of the witches' year. As I said in my last letter, these two
things are related, for the eight festivals are celebrations of
events in the Earth life of Goddess and God manifest. I can
write about both subjects in the same letter.

Not all witches understand this story in exactly the same
way. It is a poetic statement, not a chemical formula. So there
are many ways to interpret it, as with any symbol or image
sequence. You will relate to it in a way that is your own. That
way will change, in time, just as you will change. The first
understanding will be modified by intuition and experience,
with the gathering of new knowledge.

Here is my current understanding, to get you started. It
begins with a paradox. I happen to pick a new year and say,
'This is where the cycle begins.' But there is no start or finish
in a circle. And the year has a cyclical rhythm, not a linear
progression. Samhain (Hallowe'en) was the Celtic New Year
and it is celebrated as such by most witches. The winter
solstice is another obvious contender. But the festival to
which it is most easy to relate for a new start is Imbolg. It is
early spring. The very first of fresh new growth is just
beginning. The Goddess is young again, virgin, and the God,
reborn at the winter solstice, now appears as a young man.
Their love promises all fulfilment, growth and fertility. At the
next festival, the spring equinox, light and dark will be
equally balanced, day and night of equal length, but the light
is waxing. Here, the Young God 'breaks the chains of winter',
finally.

Now they are pledged to each other and their sexual union
brings all life into a new balance.

30

At Beltane, the May Eve festival which follows on from the spring equinox in the annual cycle, the Goddess and God are 'married'.

Of course, it is impossible that the Goddess should be anyone's wife in a Christian sense. But that is not what is meant. Rather, they become bonded as true partners, in love. For love exists as a subjective and objective fact, and the ultimate in all of our psychic-emotional range of experience. Love is of the Goddess. And it is also of the God, in his role as the young Eros, ecstatic, with that blend of reverence and desire which both transforms and renews. When love is genuine, it is both impersonal, recognizing the god or goddess in every man or woman, and it is intensely personal, being centred intimately on the one beloved. At Beltane, then, God and Goddess are 'married'.

Paradoxically, in the past, this festival was celebrated in orgies by Pagans. Sexual love, desire, both the personal and the impersonal kind. Can we know either type of love in its purest essence if we have not experienced the other type? I do not think so.

In folklore, the Goddess turns into a white hart on May Eve. The young God is a hunter. He pursues her into the forest and catches her. She turns, at bay, and becomes a beautiful woman. He makes love to her and dies of love in her arms, to be instantly reborn, but as a changed being. The Goddess, too, is changed, for she is now fruitful. Life and creativity are ensured.

Sexual imagery is the strongest recurrent theme in witchcraft. It is the witches' main symbol of integration. In this image, the witch seeks to harmonize with the natural flow of life, as well as to reconcile the intuitive and the rational, the inner and the outer, the passive and the active, within his or her own nature. For this is the inner marriage of Sun and Moon. Sex is also stressed because it is the means by which we enter life. To a witch, therefore (I will say it again, it is worth saying), sexuality is sacred. Sexual pleasure is a true celebration of life, an act of worship. It is the mystery, the force behind the stars.

31

Perhaps this is the moment to explain more fully the nature of both God and Goddess. As I have said, the God is often depicted as half man and half beast, being strongly sexual, wild, untamed and wise. He is, in fact, the Father of All Life, Father Nature.

He was always known as the God of the countryside, and worshipped by the country people in many guises and under many names. Among these, were the Greek Pan, with his horns and cloven hoofs, and the Celtic Cernunnos, or English Herne, with antlers. He should really be thought of as instinctive life energy. In the realm beyond life, he is guardian and guide, and one of his many names is Lord of Death, the death that leads on to rebirth. Whilst the Goddess is a trinity of persons, three in one, the God is two. As God of the waxing year and God of the waning year, his two selves are reconciled by love of the Goddess. This keeps them in relationship, one to the other.

He is also Lord of Day and Lord of Night. As Lord of Day, he is young, strong, virile, a hunter who takes with gratitude only that which is needed. In recent times, the native American men, the Red Indians, have lived this aspect of him thoroughly enough to have become the archetypal example within western culture. Once, all men lived like that, and then, perhaps, it could be said that the Horned One truly walked on Earth. The Lord of Night is a wiseman, tribal shaman. He understands the mysteries and can heal wounds. Poet, storyteller, teacher and spellcaster, his inner core is wisdom and he can transcend all boundaries, including the one between life and death. His spirit travels.

Any man may express or manifest either side or both sides of the God, if he is at one with life and reconciled within himself. Then his life will be lived as priest and son of the Horned God. Of course, in our culture, the Horned God is not acknowledged, so there is no encouragement given to men who are determined to do this. For the Horned God is not interested in capital or profit, still less in the rape or domination of either women or the whole natural world. He is interested in joyful sex, play, mischief, music, dance and the inner quest for wisdom. He just likes being alive. His way was followed when the world was much younger, when humankind lived in ecological balance with nature. When the Triple Goddess was worshipped universally.

Witchcraft is a Goddess-centred religion. I should, perhaps, have begun with a description of her qualities. (Not that I can ever 'sum up' either deity: it would be like trying to put life inside a box.) But the Horned One may, perhaps, need more explanation, for it is he, the Goatfoot, half man and half beast, to whom the Christians turned for a 'scapegoat'. They turned his imagery of horns and cloven hooves and strong sexuality into their idea of the Devil, principle of evil. And now the world is worse than grey without the Horned One and his laughter, freedom, happy, honest lustfulness and music. It is a terrible and dangerous thing when men are on hostile terms with the life force, secretly or openly hating their bodies, women's bodies and the Earth itself, and hiding behind their credit cards, their fast cars and missiles. The Horned One has no hatred. He is constantly fulfilled by his own dance of life, his own part in creation. If the Goddess is the ground of our being, he is that which surges forth, travels and yet returns to her, enriched with loving wisdom. If she is silence and peace, then song and dance are the Horned One's domain. He is joyful and always free. For women, he is the 'inner male', somewhat like the animus described by Carl Jung. For men, he is that which moves their very bones to action.

The Goddess, the threefold creator of life, has been known by many names. To some witches, she is called Aradia. She is also known as Bride, Diana, Ashtoreth, Marian, Artemis and Ceridwen. As Mother Earth, she is called Gaia. To list all of her names would take too long, but they are found in the myths and folk stories of every land. You may name her 'Great Goddess' or 'Mother' or 'Lady of Wisdom' – whatever seems right to you. She was worshipped throughout the prehistoric world and is always with us, even when we do not worship or acknowledge her. For the Goddess, like the God, is not an abstraction, in whom we need to 'have faith'. But unlike him, she contains and sustains us, constantly. She is the felt essence at the heart of things. We meet her in rocks, trees, pools, oceans, all living creatures. And her mystery is that which we perceive, the one we can feel. She is not only the Moon in its three phases, but also Mother Earth and all the expressions of the Moon on Earth; and she is the whole infinite host of the stars. Above all, she is the spirit within all these things, and the essence of peace and wholeness within each one of us.

She is also the process of death which makes way for new life. She is death-in-life, as well as life-in-death, for in her these opposites are reconciled as the Circle of Rebirth. In her, all things shift shape, all change is made, through the constantly moving and every varying dance of life.

She is the ground of our being, in so far as we can ever know it. Most often, she is seen as Goddess of the Moon, or of the Moon on Earth, because of the Moon's connection with female cycles and with the processes of conception, generation and birth; also, because the Moon shines for us at night, time of mystery, poetry, enchantment and dreams, time of intuition, the wisdom of femaleness.

The first of her three phases is that of Maid. She is the untamed, unstructured beginning of life. She initiates things. Journeys into uncharted places belong to her, whether into the world or into the self. One of her names is Lady of the Wild Things. She is at home in wild places, far from the cities. Any woman can show attributes of the Maid, whatever her physical age.

The Mother is the one who brings birth. She is there whenever we complete a book or poem, song or picture; or when we fulfil a dream or see a project right through to the end. She has given birth to everything: all the worlds and all the birds and beasts, the fishes and the rocks, the trees and flowers. In sex, she is the orgasm. In life, she is fulfilment, the completion. She is primary, the source of all life. Before her there was the primal unity, that which existed, paradoxically, before all life began, and which will exist at the end of life, before rebirth. This is complete harmony, a true union of the sexes and a state of only latent possibilities. But once manifest life exists in any way, then the Mother of Life has brought forth. Prehistoric figurines show her with pregnant belly and huge breasts, squatting to give birth. These emphasize the blood and milk of motherhood, the physical reality and the immense power, along with the nurturing and tending qualities.

The Crone, the Old Wisewoman, is about earth wisdom and star wisdom. She is the distillation of all experience and intuition. She can heal. She knows about herbs. She also knows all the mysteries. Therefore, she sees patterns, knows the future and can give advice. Inner knowing, skill in trance, divination and psychism are all hers. She brings an end to things, clearing away the outworn to make way for new life. She is the power of the waning Moon. In her, we look for knowledge of the roots of things, or draw our own power back down to our own roots, as a plant does in the winter.

But there are not three Goddesses. Rather, there is one, the Triple Goddess, three in one. For she is simultaneously each of the above three phases.

So, after this long pause at Beltane, I will go on with the story of the year's eight festivals, which show the Goddess and the God creating and sustaining life and bringing change together. In reality, to talk of either of them separately, is a bit like talking of the night without the day, or vice-versa.

At the summer solstice, a peak of fulfilment is reached. In this moment, the tide turns. The God is a man at the height of his strength and virility, and the Goddess is Queen of Summer. They have reached the full culmination of an outward flowering. They are a man and a woman at the peak of their physical love and perfection. Nevertheless, the Sun of this great celebration, as well as of the Earthly year, will now begin to wane, and the inward journey to the realm of afterlife, the 'Summerlands', has now begun. Therefore, the God is inwardly transformed. 'He has set sail for the Isle of Rebirth', is how this change is spoken of and symbolized. Outwardly, in nature, his power now goes into the grain, as the Sun ripens what Mother Earth is producing.

The Goddess is all beauty and abundance at this time. She presides over the God's transformation for it happens through love of her. And it is in their shared ecstacy that he becomes his other self. She is fulfilment, the green leaves and many-coloured flowers of high summer, and all enjoyment, love and passion. She simply is, abundantly, and in her, we are fulfilled.

At Lammas (Lughnasadh) the Goddess gives birth. It is the festival of the First Fruits of the Harvest. The God again dies for the Goddess. His power has gone into the corn and now it begins to be reaped, for the Goddess must take his energy, his life, that new life can be born. She becomes 'the Implacable One, the Grim Reaper' as well as the Abundant Mother, Lady of the Harvest. The God, after his sacrifice as Corn King, is reborn, the bread of life. (The Christian story of death, resurrection and the bread which is the body, is a particular variation of this, the original story.) And the images this time are burial and birth, as well as bread. A sacrifice so that life may go on.

In ancient times, the God's sacrifice was sometimes enacted by the actual killing of a man, but this is thought by some to have been done only at those periods of history (or pre-history) when Pagan practice had departed from its original purity and become decadent. The evidence of myth and legend shows that the sacrifice was often (and perhaps originally) a substitute for a man, in the shape of an animal or image. And in Ireland, there was a legend surrounding the burial of a man up to his neck in earth for three days at Lughnasadh. On the third day, he was released. However gently this festival is celebrated in modern times, there is evidence that blood was often spilled in the past, but not the rivers of blood demanded in modern warfare as a sacrifice to the god of money. (For it is arms dealers who profit in any war.)

At Mabon, autumn equinox, we meet the Lord and Lady of Abundance. This is the Harvest Festival. They are surrounded by the fruits of their lives and their love. Now light and dark are once again in balance, but the light is waning. The God is a great deal older than he was at the spring equinox. This is a time of reckoning as well as of thanksgiving. This is the harvest as against the loss, a time of weighing up and looking back, from the perspective of mature judgement. Wisdom must be called upon to make these assessments. Now, the Sun King has become the Lord of Shadows. Nevertheless, the Goddess gives us laden tables and full barns and cupboards at this time. There is fruit on the trees for birds, and animals gather their winter stores, from what she has provided. This is a festival of celebration, a thanksgiving.

At the festival of Samhain (Hallowe'en) we begin the New Year. We end in the beginning, and we begin in the end. This is the Festival of the Returning Dead. The gates of life and death and those between the worlds are open. The living may meet with the dead and the unborn, to exchange love and information, if they so wish. Witches don't 'call back' the dead. They regard this as a wrong thing to do. The dead are not, and should never be, at our beck and call, for death involves many stages, processes of both purification and spiritual rebalancing, and rest and deep communion with the source of all life. There may be stages of learning and preparation for new life, the next incarnation. However, on this night of the year's death, witches make a (psychic) space for the Beloved Dead to come back, if they want to and are able.

The Goddess has become the Old Crone, Wisewoman, at Samhain. She brings knowledge that may be bitter at first, but which leads on to wisdom. The God is the Lord of Death, guide through the dark days, the winter.

At the winter solstice, the whole cycle begins again. Not, as we might expect, with a progression from Old Crone to Maid, following the normal sequence of the Moon's phases. It is the darkest night. There is a pause, a waiting. Will the light be reborn? Will the Sun return? Deep, black darkness reigns, like the inside of the cauldron of the Great Mother. In this vessel of transformation, the ancient Lord of Shadows becomes the new Sun King, the newborn Child of Promise.

37

In other words, at Yuletide, all must return to the Mother (the old correlation between tomb and womb). At the Christian festival of Christmas, people still celebrate the birth of a Sun child, Jesus, the Church having chosen this time as the most appropriate for the event. And we all (as though, perhaps, obeying an ancient inner call) return to our personal mothers, to the family home. Unless, that is, we are mature women, in which case we are in some sense, mothers, welcoming and tending to our family or friends. Or unless we are mature men, supporting the mother, as her consort. But the father's role is a shadowy one, like that of the Christian Joseph. He stands, in a sense, for the year that has passed. His son/rival, God of the Waxing Year, is being born, a process acted out in many ancient mummers' performances, like that of the Marshfield Mummers, in Marshfield, Avon, each Boxing Day morning.

In personal terms, a man who is sensitive to his own inner changes may feel a reorientation towards life, during or just after the winter solstice.

For women, the experience is also one of transformation and renewal, but whereas she is actually the medium through which a man is restored to himself, reborn, when it is her turn, he simply supports and guides her in *giving birth to herself*. His role is a protective one.

And so, all having returned to the Mother, we start again. The wheel turns. At Imbolg the Maid appears, together with the young God who was born at the winter solstice.

At Yule, the winter solstice, the most magical event of all the year takes place. Within a timeless moment, all things are made new. Not only does the Lord of the Waning Year die, to be reborn as the Lord of the New Waxing Year, but the Goddess gives birth to her own younger self. All of nature is restored.

In celebrating all these festivals, keeping pace with them in our lives, we harmonize with the year. This is the natural year on whose rhythms we all depend for food and so for life (however far we may be from the countryside). Thus, we integrate with the archetypal patterns of change and growth, yearly and in a lifetime.

I have to acknowledge that my vision of the Goddess and God of the witches is exclusively heterosexual. And it is fair that you should know this, for others may comment upon it. Through this outlook, I run the risk of giving offence to some other witches, because of misunderstanding. So I must explain that since the year's mythology is about physical fruitfulness, is about nature and reproduction, it can only be about love between man and woman. Now as an image of inner and outer fruitfulness and creativity, this need not give offence, as it holds good whether individual witches are homosexual, bisexual or, as is the case with each of you heterosexual but single, or married (to someone of the opposite sex). It is not a vision relevant only to those of 'straight' sexual orientation, since it is an image of the processes of all conception and of all fruitful union of opposites.

The dates of the Sabbats (festivals) are generally agreed upon for the four 'quarters', Imbolg, Beltane, Lughnasadh and Samhain. Those for the 'cross quarters' (equinoxes and solstices) will vary from year to year. These should be checked in a current ephemeris.

Yule/winter solstice	20th–23rd December
Imbolg/Candlemas	2nd February
Eostar/spring equinox	20th–23rd March
Beltane/May Eve	30th April
Litha/summer solstice	20th–23rd June
Lughnasadh/Lammas	1st August
Mabon/autumn equinox	20th–23rd September
Samhain/Hallowe'en	31st October

I would like to make one last comment about this old knowledge kept alive in witchcraft. We may be celebrating the old festivals and calling ourselves modern Pagans (which indeed we are), but our practices are radically different from those of our forebears. We cannot help but be of the twentieth century, be what we are, if our worship is to be genuine and alive. Otherwise, our rites and ceremonies will be merely 'picturesque' and empty of all meaning. We must reinterpret old beliefs in the light of present-day knowledge of disciplines like psychology, feminist theory, environmentalism, new physics, psychic research and psycho-drama. Modern witchcraft is a new religion. It grows from the seed of the old Pagan tree, but it is not that tree, it is a new one. The old Paganism died in Europe, was killed in fact, deliberately, during the great persecution of witches (now called the Burning Times).

The basic themes of old Paganism underlie all forms of life. They are about archetypal patterns and, for that reason, the oldest of all religions had to be reborn. But within modern witchcraft, there are many new styles and approaches. My aim, as hedge witch, working independently from any coven, is to find the essence, the true spirit of the craft, in the simplest, least complicated of ways.

Anyway, I think this is enough for now.

Blessed be,
Rae

New Green
Avonford

3rd March 1987

Dear Tessa and Glyn,
    I will write next about the casting of a magic circle. If you
are a witch, this is your temple. It is an ephemeral, transitory
creation; not for us, expensive buildings, costly artefacts.
Instead, there is the circle, cast anew wherever you may be. In
a perfect world, you would often be outdoors, with a
tree-stump for your altar, and in the middle of a wood. Or
you might be on a hilltop with a big fire burning. Since life is
no longer like that for most of us, you will probably be in
your own house. Having said that, I have to say, also, that
anyone who has not looked for the Lord and Lady in the
woods and fields or in a tree or flower, or on a windy hilltop,
has missed most of the point.
    Before you cast a circle for a Full Moon Rite, go outside to
look up at the Full Moon in the sky. It is a necessary
communion. See and feel her silver light, her power, in your
heart and mind, your body and spirit.
    Back indoors, you may want to prepare with a bath or
shower. This has become a modern 'tradition'. It is a simple
rite of psychic, as well as physical cleansing. Purifying herbs,
or a handful of salt, can be added to the bath water. The bath
provides a space for transition, from the everyday to a
heightened and magical consciousness. It is a good new idea.
And it is worth putting into practice, even though it is
obvious that our forebears, lacking bathrooms, must have
prepared themselves for a rite in some other way.
    After the bath, dress in clean clothes. You should wear no
deodorant, hair gel or any chemically based perfumes. Hair
should be worn loose and all wrist-watches, hair clips and
unconsecrated jewellery should be left outside the circle,
otherwise vibrations and associations from these may disturb
your rite. Preferably, you should be dressed in a robe of
natural fibre, one that you wear for magic and for nothing

41

else. If a robe does not appeal, design your own 'working' outfit. Green is a suitable colour for natural magic. Blue is a Goddess colour. Brown reminds us of our contact with the earth and our dependence on it. (There are many excellent books on colour symbolism and this, along with herbal magic and the occult properties of natural objects and phenomena, is the kind of knowledge a witch should make his or her own.)

One tradition, for women is worth following whatever else you have or have not got on, and that is the wearing of a necklace. It links the woman with the Goddess, since it represents the circle of rebirth. Any necklace will do, as long as it is made of natural materials – pottery, glass, semi-precious stones or wooden beads are all suitable. Plastic and other inorganic substances are not, because they have no life and are poor conductors of etheric energy, and are therefore inappropriate for the working of magic.

The same rule (organic materials only) applies to all the working tools of witchcraft. The first tool is a magic knife, called an athame. This does not have to be the black-handled, narrow-bladed knife of occult tradition; a small lock-knife will do just as well; a kitchen knife is also very good. Choose one that appears at home with magic. It should, perhaps, have a 'primitive' shape and a wooden handle. Sheath knives are another possibility. Look around till you find one that fires your imagination. (It is said that you should never haggle over the price of your magic knife.) A knife that is not new may be used, if you know its history and can therefore be sure it has never been used for any kind of violence. As with all magical equipment, you should wash it and leave it in salt water for an hour or more. This will strip it of previous associations and also cleanse it magically.

Having first cleared and marked out a circle (nine feet in diameter if your room is large enough for that) you should place your altar in the circle. The altar may be a small flat-topped table or cupboard, or something that you have constructed specially. Position it at the northernmost edge, since a witch's altar should face north. This is because the power, that is, the current of Earth energy, comes from the north. It also shows a reverence for the body of life, the Goddess manifest in nature, since, in magical belief, north is the direction corresponding to earthly existence.

On your altar, you can place your athame, some incense (or joss-sticks), two candles, a small bowl of water and a stone. You will also need bread and wine, with a chalice for the communion. In the centre of the circle, there should be a large ironware, black enamel or pottery cooking-pot, representing the cauldron. This may hold water, herbs, a candle, flowers, or whatever suits the particular rite.

The items that you use for working magic are both symbolic and of actual etheric vitality. Their meaning comes from far back in time. They are of the four elements, from whose expression, interweaving and existence all life finds form and being. When the Goddess builds life, these are her raw materials, the elements. And each one is presided over by elemental spirits, guardians. They represent different levels or areas of life. Air for the mind, Fire for the vital energy (electricity), the life spark or leyline, Water for soul or emotions, Earth for the physical body. The cauldron represents a fifth element. Ether, or realm of spirit. This is the vessel of the Great Mother, Herself, in which all transformation takes place. Think of it as the All, and Nothing. There, anything can happen. It is pure transcendence, the point where conscious understanding stops. And it is represented by a cauldron (cooking-pot), because the cooking of food is a process of change, the most basic alchemy. The cauldron is the mystery of all creation. All the other elements are brought to birth, sustained and upheld by the fifth, Ether.

I have said these symbols are about knowledge from way back. This is shown in mythology, where the four 'treasures' representing elements are usually a sword, a wand or spear, a cup and a stone. Similarly, a pack of tarot cards is based on recognition of the elements, with swords, wands, cups and pentacles showing Air, Fire, Water and Earth (while the fifth, Ether, appears in the cards as the major arcanum). Astrology also recognizes the four elements, and comprehends the entire essence of any chart, the whole *Gestalt*, as the fifth, the spirit. Each one of these traditions shares with modern witchcraft origins in the Pagan occult knowledge.

Light the candles and the incense. Walk deosil – clockwise, the direction of building and creating – around the circle, pointing your knife firmly at the circle's edge. Imagine that blue light is streaming from the point of your knife. It will actually be doing so, whether you can see it or not, as what we imagine has true astral reality, and appears in that realm which can be seen by psychics and clairvoyants. Visualize the blue light filling up all the space around your circle, creating an effect like the skin of an orange, only much thicker, so that you are still within it, even when standing at the outermost edges of the circle. You are enclosed in a blue sphere. Walk round three times, stating that you draw the circle in the names of the Triple Goddess of the Circle of Rebirth and of the Horned God, both as a container of sacred powers, and as a protection. Replace your knife on the altar.

Next, take the incense round (deosil) and offer it up, by raising it high at the easternmost point of your circle. (You will need a compass to have checked these directions, earlier.) As you do so, request the Guardian Spirits of the East, Blessed Spirits of Air, to witness your rites and protect your circle. Continue round the circle, clockwise, and place the incense on the ground at the east point.

Take one of the candles round. (The other is your altar candle.) Offer it at the southern point and say there, *I call upon the Guardian Spirits of the South, Blessed Spirits of Fire, to witness these rites and to protect this circle.* Carry the candle on round and then return it to the south. Place it on the ground.

Repeat the same procedure with the water, offering it at the west, to the Guardian Spirits of the West, Blessed Spirits of Water. Then take the stone around deosil, offering it high above the altar, to the Guardian Spirits of the North, of Earth.

Replace your knife upon the altar, saying, *The circle is cast.* Now you are in a complete magic circle and may worship and work magic free from psychic interruption. If, for any reason, you must leave the circle during a rite, carve an imaginary door in the blue sphere with your athame and then step through, remembering to close the door behind you. Open and close the door again when you go back in, using the athame to make ritual, symbolic gestures. Visualize the door clearly. In the world of magic, what you imagine has vivid, psychic reality.

Most traditions of witchcraft include the casting of a magic circle in this or some other way. It can be done more informally, by a simple demarcation of the circle with stones, shells or a long white cord. Invocations to the four quarters, can be made using an improvised poem, spoken to the powers of Air, Fire, Water and Earth, at each corresponding point. (There is no need to take incense or anything around the circle, though you, yourself, must still proceed deosil.) The four quarters could be marked by a feather, a wand, a dish of water or else a shell, and a stone or else a dish of salt.

Magic has been made elaborate, concerned with virgin parchment, special signs and sigils, learned invocations. But if you are a hedge witch it can be direct, spontaneous. It can be an easy connection between the witch, her/his inner guides and the environment. Whatever the methods and whatever the symbols, the principle is that of creating space 'between the worlds', the sacred space.

Visualization, what you see with the 'mind's eye', is at the heart of all magic. Without this, there is no life, the spell falls flat, for what has not been created on inner levels, cannot be made manifest, in any sense. Without visualization, no magical act can take effect, however proficient, technically, the working. To cast a circle, you picture each element and see the energy, see living shapes.

At the east, see rushing winds, sunrise, the clear bright skies of a spring morning. Feel the essence of all air, the breath of life, inspiration.

At the south, see flames, gold, orange, red, the noon-day summer Sun. Feel heat, the sensuality of southern climates, the vital dance of fire, of all energy, of the creative outflow of life, passion.

At the west, see waves, water, silver sea's edge in an autumn twilight. Feel the poetry, the power of enchantment, the imagination.

At the north, see dark earth, the secrecy of roots and seeds, in winter. Inwardness, containing all Earth life. See midnight, under the North Star. See mountains, minerals, the great age and the groundedness of manifest life, both mystery and great abundance.

The Ether may be visualized as a dream, or as the night sky or a crucible. Or as darkness, bearing an infinitesimal point of light. Images may suggest themselves to you. In some traditions, Ether is symbolized by a cord, because a cord binds, weaves. When visualizing Ether, you may see the web of life, a woman weaving, or a single thread. Ether has no special time or season, because it is everywhere and nowhere. Feel the essence of fate in the whole complex pattern of life, the profound connections.

The tools which you use for magic should be consecrated, as should any jewellery, or clothes. Since that is done at the time of self-initiation, I will describe it in a future letter.

After the rite has ended, take the incense at the East and offer it again, thanking the Spirits of the East for their protection and blessing, and then saying, *Hale and farewell*. The incense is then taken round (still deosil) and returned to the altar. The candles, water and stone are likewise taken round, and the Spirits of Fire, Water and Earth thanked for protection and blessing, concluding with the words, *Hale and farewell*. Do not omit this. The Guardian Spirits will continue to protect you only if you treat them with courtesy, and that includes telling them you are thankful for their blessing, and are now ending your rite. (The blue sphere, unlike the Guardian Spirits, is of your creation. It will naturally fade on its own, once you have ceased to imagine it is there.)

Finally, the altar candles are extinguished. Tradition has something to say about this too. They should be pinched or snuffed out, never blown. And the incense should be left to burn until it is finished, as putting out the incense is said to be a symbol of putting out the breath of life.

One more word about the elements. The fifth, which is Ether, gives birth to the four and sustains them. Its place in the circle is the point at the absolute centre, *and* it is the circumference. Thus, it is said to be 'everywhere and nowhere, within and without, throughout and about'. It is both immanence and transcendence. Air is the province of knowledge, Fire of will; Water is the emotions, the capacity to feel; Earth is the body of life, full, incarnate and sensate being.

These four quarters, each linked with the fifth, make the pattern of an equal-armed cross within a circle; the Pagan mandala which predates Christianity.

The five elements can also be seen represented in the five-point star which is the emblem of witchcraft. The fifth, uppermost point is Ether, Spirit, while the other four are Air, Fire, Earth and Water. This symbol, the pentacle, represents our religion to us, as the cross represents Christianity. The pentacle, enclosed within a circle, is often worn by witches as a pendant and is usually displayed upon the altar in some shape or form.

That's enough for now. Bright blessings on your future rites, and on your learning, both.

Blessed be,
Rae

New Green
Avonford

16th March 1987

Dear Tessa and Glyn,

It is almost the spring equinox, and we have had equinoctial gales, as no doubt you will have noticed! You, like nature, may have felt chaotic, wild. The two weeks before and after both equinoxes are often times of stress and great tension. This is because all the elements of life are being brought into new balance, psychically, as day and night attain equal length. At the spring equinox, light is gaining, for future days will now be longer than the nights. So a new tide of life begins. But first the old ways must be broken down. Times of transition are, potentially, both stressful and chaotic. Out of this chaos, new ways arise. It isn't always easy to believe it at the time, but from a breaking-up, new life comes.

Therefore, the main spring-equinox or Eostar symbol is the egg, which symbolizes fertility in nature. It also shows how plans that were being hatched on the inner levels during the winter may now be put into practice in our lives. We may take the first steps towards doing something we have only dreamt about. (This powerful symbol is still retained in the folk memory, as Eostar eggs are still popular with everyone.)

Eggs, hardboiled and perhaps hand-painted for decoration, should be on the altar. They show the emergence of life from darkness, of ideas from inner levels. They are the Goddess fertile, rich with promise and potential life. Not for nothing is this festival named Eostar, but for the ancient Teutonic Goddess Oestre, whose name connects with the root of our modern world oestrogen, the hormone stimulating ovulation.

After the casting of the circle, invoke the Lady and the Lord. This is the Festival of New Life. Now the winter is finally left behind, along with what belongs to winter. The Goddess is Spring Maiden and the God is young, the ardent one. Their union brings all life into new order. Now things are different. Spring flowers appear on the Earth, where the

Goddess walks. And the beasts of the field and wood, the birds of the air, prepare to bring forth young.

There is the breaking of shells, pushing through earth, growth of new buds, hatching, the richness of eggs. Heat. Fertility. This is the Festival of the New Balance, as the Sun gains strength.

After the invocation, dance deosil around the circle. On this occasion, you should sing about new life, change. It could be something like this.

> *Breaking through and breaking out.*
> *Change! Sun and Earth together,*
> *pledged for life, within, without,*
> *Sun God stretches out his hand,*
> *Spring Queen dances through the land.*
> *Spring blooms, throughout and about.*

Visualize the energy created by your dance as a golden cone of light. Direct this into the cauldron, at the centre of the circle, using the power of your thought. Now light a third candle, which should be inside the cauldron. As you light it, say, *I light this candle to the Sun.*

Also inside the cauldron, around the candle, there should be spring flowers. Take them out and hold them high above the altar. Say, *May the blessing of the Spring Queen be upon these flowers, the fresh bloom of new life.*

Take some of the flowers to the east quarter. Offer them up, saying, *May there be new understanding on Earth, new awareness and knowledge of Mother Earth's needs. As spring flowers bloom afresh, may this blossom.*

Lay the flowers on the ground beside the incense.

Return to the altar for more flowers (deosil) and take them to the south, offering them up with these, or similar words: *May there be a return of joy in life. In song, dance, love, and the beauty of all the natural world. May this blossom.*

Lay the flowers on the ground beside the candle. Return to the altar.

Take flowers to the west in offering. Say, *May there be peace on Earth. May this blossom.*

Lay the flowers on the ground beside the water. Return to the altar.

Take flowers all the way around the circle, from north back to north again. Offer these up, saying, *May the greenwoods return, the freedom and balance of natural life. May this blossom.*

Lay the flowers on the ground, before the altar. Sit beside the cauldron. Visualize the blossoming of new awareness, joy in life and peace, and the greenwoods returning. People in harmony with each other and with all life forms on the Earth. See this flowering across the world, the sight and scent of this encouraged, stimulated, by the return of spring flowers. If the image seems too fragile, remember flowers can even break up concrete. After the rite, you can gather them up again, and keep them in a vase.

And that is the spring-flower spell.

Take one of the eggs from the bowl on the altar. Hold it on high, saying, *Blessed be, the life from within life.*

Go to the centre of the circle and sit by the cauldron again. This time, curl your body, tuck in your head, as though inside an eggshell. You are in your egg space and you are about to hatch out. Think of the egg you held at the altar. Life is enclosed, growing inside the darkness of a shell. Your winter self has been like that. Your winter plans have been incubating slowly. Feel the life of these new plans, frail but determined. Feel the new person you have become because of them, newly ready to emerge into the Sun. And visualize yourself reaching out to break through your shell, breaking out, shell shattering. You step out, new self, into a new phase of your life. Now the old way has been lost. The elements of life must be brought into new balance.

Go to each of the quarters in turn. First the east. Sit quietly with eyes closed and think about your mind, your mental state and attitudes. Ask the Spirits of Air to guide your thoughts, so that you may achieve new harmony of mind. Listen carefully for any inner messages and remember any images you may see with your 'mind's eye'. These may be important and you will understand them later, if not at the time. Do not try to analyse them.

Now go to the south quarter. Sit quietly and ask the Guardian Spirits of Fire for guidance on vitality and change. Again, listen and watch for any messages. Remember, the south is also the quarter of passion.

Visit also the west and the north, asking the Spirits of Water for guidance on harmony of emotions and the Spirits of Earth about a physical harmony. Listen and watch for messages.

Well, that's all the magical work for the Spring Equinox, unless you also want to consecrate all the eggs in the bowl, and give them as Eostar gifts to your family and friends.

Lay your hands over the bowl and say, *May these be blessed and consecrated, in the names of the Spring Queen and her consort, the Young God.*

Take the bowl deosil around the circle, passing it through the smoke of incense and the (south) candle flame, sprinkling it with water and, at the north, touching the bowl to the stone.

Say, *May those who receive these be rich with new, fertile life. May their dreams become reality, and their plans be blessed by the Sun.*

Bless the bread and wine and end with communion. Then thank the Lord and Lady for their blessing, bidding them, *Hale and farewell.* Open your circle.

Blessings on your Eostar celebrations.

Blessed Be,
Rae

New Green
Avonford

16th April 1987

Dear Tessa and Glyn,

It is time I wrote about Moon celebrations. For the Triple Goddess of the Circle of Rebirth is, in fact, Triple Goddess of the Moon. She is also of the Earth and stars, the Mother of All Life, but it is through the Moon that we relate to her most easily. Moonlight means enchantment, intuition, poetry. Simply to look at the Moon with a poet's eye is to see the Goddess. The connection between Moon phases and women's menstrual cycles is an obvious and potent fact. In witchcraft, therefore, the Full Moon celebrations (Esbats) are as important as the Sabbats.

We do not always formally celebrate all three phases of each Moon cycle, because we can worship the Goddess in her three aspects at the Full Moon. This is the time of the Mother, but we can acknowledge the Maid and the Mother and Crone that she has been and is and will be. There are not three Goddesses but one, three in one.

Full Moon is the high tide of psychic power and of fulfilment, time of worship and of celebration. To honour and to celebrate the Goddess between the worlds is itself an invocation that her worship be seen once more on the Earth, and that the Goddess shall return to the people and the people to her. Then the old ways would prevail again. The old love of poetry and magic would reign, the respect and love for Mother Earth, and a knowledge of the sacredness of sexual love; therefore an end to competitive, exploitative and ruthless values. At Full Moon, then, the Goddess and her fully blossomed beauty and enchantment are invoked, for change.

Full Moon is the time of consummation and the peak of power. In ordinary life, it can be the last straw in unstable situations. Feelings can erupt when change is realized. But the Full Moon can also bring emotional fulfilment. And you may

53

notice that any special visitors or important letters frequently arrive at this time. It is good for magical pilgrimages and for love and for any kind of celebration.

A man does not have any outer bodily sign, linking him to Moon rhythms. He has no Moon-flow of blood. But a male witch understands the Moon through awareness of a monthly cycle of moods, psychological rhythm and psychic attunement in his own soul. Any man may well have a surge of extra energy at Full Moon (unless he is overtired, when sudden exhaustion is more likely). At Full Moon a man can realize his needs. He can invoke, by poetry or dance or music, or by ritual, for their fulfilment. He can also, like the female witch, *be* fulfilled. The sense of at-oneness with the Goddess's Moon tides may come to him psychically, or through love, passion, art, celebration or the realization of a dream.

After casting the circle, as usual, and invoking the Goddess as *Silver Lady, bright Mistress of all love and enchantment*, you should also invoke the Horned God. While she is ethereal, graceful, and yet sings in our blood and in all the physical rhythms of sex and childbirth, he is primitive, wild, shaggy-thighed, and yet sings with the hunter's subtlety and the storyteller's magic. Their presence can be sensed and produces awe, a joyful wonder.

Your cauldron should be filled with water for this rite. Place it at the centre of your circle.

Stand before the altar and read or speak this, or something like it: *This is the time of Full Moon, high tide of psychic power. Plants grow and tides change and man and woman join in desire, passion. Change is made and realized and dreams are revealed. I dance in a ring to honour the Triple Goddess of the Moon, her infinite changes and returning phases; calm and passionate, serene and wild; the dance of life.*

Dance deosil around the circle, singing,

> *Moon dance of life*
> *with silver song*
> *in vein and river,*

silver song in dark night –
now work enchantment, fill the world
with power of magic, full unfurled.
Now magic grow, enchantment flow.
I dance the silver tide's return,
by breath and blood, by water and bone.

Direct the power into the waters of your cauldron. Then sprinkle water upon the floor within your circle, saying,

Silver dew fall gently, bring peace and beauty.
As between the worlds, so in the world.

Drink some of the water from your cupped hand. And say,

The blessings of the Triple Goddess of the Moon
are life, love and skills of magic.
Thus, I invoke her with these words:
'Blessed be! all who
dance, give and take
pleasure and dream enchantment
into being, with harm to none,
and in her sacred name. Blessed be!

Pause, and say, *As on my lips, so on all lips.*

Next, take a pipe or whistle. This may be of wood, but a metal 'penny whistle' will do well. It is certainly the God's instrument in Britain, though in Greece he plays the pan-pipes and in India, a bamboo flute. Reed and bone whistles were made in neolithic times, and whistles of various kinds still exist everywhere.

Because of their shape and the likeness of their sound to birdsong, they were used magically in the past, and they still are.

Say, *On this night, the Horned God draws near to the Moon Goddess, that they may be one, in love. I play this pipe to honour him, all his wild music. As the music ripples on bright water, so may the male and female be reconciled in love, in the world, to the Earth's healing and to the happiness of all creatures.*

Play the pipe, imagining the notes falling into the cauldron, and there rippling, silver-bright. All the water is charged with the God's music. As you play, hear the sweet echo of the Horned God's playing, wilder and far more pure, from behind your own notes. Visualize the power of love (which does exist, against all odds) the power of fulfilment in love to bring healing and happiness, the effect of love spreading out in ripples.

Don't worry if you can't play the pipe like a skilled musician. A few notes, repeated, are all you need. Play with the pipe, seeing what kind of sound you can make if you approach it with fun.

Replace the pipe upon the altar. Now take a silver ring. This need not be expensive, but should not have been used for any other purpose previously. It should have been bought especially for magic. Before the rite, it should also have been cleaned, and then immersed in salt water for at least one hour, to cleanse it psychically.

Dip the ring into the waters of the cauldron. Then, holding it in your two hands, sit and dream about three wishes you would now like the Moon Goddess to grant. Picture them, one by one, coming true. Take your time over this. Think carefully about the consequences, remembering 'Harm none' as the first and only rule of magic, and life.

It is a good idea to follow tradition and wish once for the world, once for a friend and once for yourself. Your wishes could then be, for example:

Peace on Earth

and

That —— [a friend's name] *may recover peace of mind*

and

A resolution of my inner conflict about —— [a moral dilemma, a relationship, etc.]

These wishes have a common theme, the return of peace, which does make concentration easier, and allows meditation and vision to flow. As you make each wish, name it out loud and give three turns to the ring, deosil. Then give the matter into the hands of the Goddess. Never wear the ring as costume jewellery.

The above is an example of the kind of thing you may do at the Full Moon. But I could never tell all that there is to tell about this celebration, let alone all there is to know about witchcraft, in these letters. *I* do not even know all there is to know, and I never will, and nor will anyone.

A Full Moon rite should end with a communion, a meal of consecrated wine and bread, or cakes. Then the Goddess and God should be thanked and bade *Hale and farewell*, and the circle opened. Keep a record of the wishes that you made, or of any other spells cast, or visions seen. This reference book is known among witches as the 'Book of Shadows'. It is a private fund of knowledge and experience. Anything useful can go into it: a herbal remedy for a sore throat, the description of a trance or dream, a way of doing link-breaking magic, love spells, healing spells, or anything. Choose the best and stoutest notebook you can find for this. It may be very old before you have finished with it, as it can be kept for reference permanently.

The traditional colour for the cover of the book is black. This indicates secrecy. It should not be shown to anyone except another witch. If you can't find any black notebooks, or if you prefer another colour, then have whatever you really want. I have had several black ones, but my current one is brown. I have also had red and blue ones. As you can see, I get through a lot of them, since mine doubles as a magical diary. Anyway, what matters is not the colour or size, but that you should feel comfortable with it.

I do not know where the name 'Book of Shadows' came from but I think there are two possibilities. One is that it relates to work done usually in shadows; that is, secretly by candlelight. The other may be an acknowledgement of the fact that a description of a charm or invocation can never be more than a shadow of the real thing.

Rites of the Moon can be worked at other phases. She does not have to be full. New Moon rites are sacred to the Maid, or Virgin Goddess. Magic done at such times is for the affirmation of the untamed aspects of the self, and for celebration of freedom. It is also done, on the New or Waxing Moon, for anything which needs to be begun, launched, built up or restored. This is the time of invocation. In life, it is a good time to begin a course of studies, to plant seeds, to start a business or to receive inspiration. An invocation on the New Moon might be this:

The Moon is New. I honour the Maid, Virgin Goddess, she who returns to her people bringing inspiration. She is untamed, the Lady of the Wild Things. Hills, moorland and deep forest are her domain. In her, we break free, we begin anew, returning to ourselves. I ask her blessing and her presence.

Waning or Dark Moon rites are sacred to the Crone, the Old Wisewoman. (The Moon is said to be Dark for the three days before the New Moon, when it has waned so far that it can no longer be seen in the sky. New Moon rites are best held three days after the actual New Moon night, when the first crescent Moon of the new cycle is visible.) Magic done when the Moon is waning is for guidance and understanding, the attainment of wisdom. It is also done to break psychic links or to rid oneself of unwanted characteristics or compulsions. This is the time of banishing. In life, it is right for honest self-assessment or for rewriting or reworking. For anything which requires objective criticism. It is also a good time to break bad habits or to leave anything unwanted or outgrown behind. An invocation on the Waning Moon might be this:

The Moon wanes. I call upon the Crone, Old Wisewoman, she who brings true vision. She is wise in the ways of all creatures and knows roots, herbs, all healing potions, whatever may be needed. She sees patterns and dreams in the glowing logs, in steam that rises from the cauldron, and in quiet waters. She can foretell, forewarn and guide. In her, we see and understand; we bring the story to its rightful end; and we gain wisdom. I ask her blessing and her presence.

(When the Horned One is invoked on the Waning Moon, as consort to the Old Wisewoman, he is, of course, the Lord of Night, Old Wiseman.)

One last word about spell-casting. Once people know that you are a witch, they may ask why you can't conjure up anything you want, any time you like. You may, yourself, have wondered why there are limits. Spell-casting is a skill, like any other. It does not work beyond or outside the laws of life. It stays well within them. In this respect, it is like weaving or woodwork. You may successfully have more than one piece of work in progress, more than one rug or item of furniture currently being worked on. But they all take time and effort and if you tried to work on 300 things at once, you couldn't do it. Like anything else, magic requires preparation and assembly of the right materials and time and then (most particularly, in this case) attainment of the right psychic state. This last is vitally important, because it can't be turned on and off anywhere and everywhere. Whilst it will always be available in an emergency, it will undoubtedly fail if you try casting spells to prove points or to entertain. It can't be lived all the time, or you would be unbalanced. Therefore, you must choose your magical priorities. Magic is a part of the flow of life. It is a kind of dance and a kind of prayer.

Blessings on all your rites of the Moon,
Rae

New Green
Avonford

24th April 1987

Dear Tessa and Glyn,

Already it is nearly Beltane. I hope this will get to you in time. The fine weather we have been having this spring makes Beltane, the time of union and pleasure, seem a lot more appropriate than it does when cold winds blow all day on 30th April – and all through May. Now it is warm, the Sun shines, there is blossom on all the trees. It is just right. Even if it rains on May Eve, we have already had a promise of summer.

To our Pagan ancestors 1st May was the first day of summer. They celebrated on the eve of May Day, with dancing, feasting and, in some cases, a full invocation for fertility. This was a 'greenwood marriage' and was understood to be a union in which the Horned God, through the medium of the man, impregnated the Goddess, through the medium of the woman. It was undertaken for the celebration of both life and love and to ensure fertility and fruitfulness in fields and among the animals and in the human tribe. Many young people would go into the forest together where, apart from making love, it was also customary to stay up all night, to watch the rising sun appear at the dawn of summer. All this was, of course, much frowned upon by the Church, when Christianity became the official religion in Britain. But the Beltane Rites remained popular with ordinary people. They were pleasurable and were felt to be vitally important to the well-being of the Earth. As the Christian years went by, however, the sexual enactment of the Sun's union with Mother Earth became symbolic, rather than literal. Maypoles and hobby-horses and garlands and dances, all the May Day pageantry, continued, while the greenwood marriages did not (at least, not officially). Then the rise of Puritanism discouraged even these more respectable forms of celebration, except in remote places. Maypoles have long

since been allowed back onto the village green, and are now part of the modern May fair, though few people understand what they mean in terms of sexual symbolism. Thus, in the past, was the God (who must be understood as Father of Life, whether in the guise of Sun King or Horned God) symbolically joined in union with the Goddess. The dancers connected themselves and their village to the web of magical energy that was created.

No one nowadays would invoke for an increase in the population of their town or village, but seen as a metaphor, the harmonious and fulfilling sexual union between the Lord and Lady is the clearest statement witchcraft can make about the way to happiness. It is about the reconciliation of all opposites in love, and the fruitfulness that arises from this. Fertility, too, can be seen as a metaphor for all kinds of things. It does not have to be about crops and babies. Even so, there are many mouths unfed, in our modern world – and many endangered species.

I hope this is not too confusing. The spirituality of pleasure is an alien concept in our present culture, but it is the theme of the Beltane Rite: innocent pleasure in sensuality, and the creativity which arises from union of opposites.

So what can you do, short of setting up a maypole in your living-room? If either of you were in a magical partnership, the answer should be obvious by now. And sometimes it can be that simple. But Beltane Rites which culminate in complete sexual union are usually happier if more informal, that is, if they take place outside the circle. There was nothing formal about the greenwood, after all.

A solitary witch, after casting a circle and invoking the presence of the Goddess and the God, could first dance and chant to raise power for magical activities, and then earth the power into an unlit candle which would be in the cauldron, at the centre of the circle. The chant could be this one, which I wrote a year or two ago, or something of your own.

Beltane

> *I dance delight*
> *on Beltane's night.*
> *All senses freeing,*
> *I dance for being.*
> *The flower and the flame*
> *of love's own rite*
> *shall blossom. Sun*
> *embrace Earth, bright.*

Light the candle to the Sun. This is your Beltane fire, your substitute for the big bonfire you could have had blazing on some hilltop if we lived in more open and accepting times. Kindling the Bel fire is an invocation to the Sun God to bring blessing and protection for the coming year. This fire, traditionally, has many healing and purifying properties. In the past, cattle were driven through the dying embers to banish diseases. Pregnant women leapt over it, if not too far advanced in pregnancy, to ensure a safe delivery. Travellers would jump the fire for a safe journey. Ill people left their diseases in the flames. Others might simply make a wish as they jumped. Couples could jump the fire together, to protect their union and to bring them luck in marriage. As you light the candle, be aware of its power and significance. State, *I light this candle to the Sun.*

Next, take a dish of earth. Bless it in the name of the Goddess. Lay your hands upon it, and say, *I bless, consecrate and set apart this earth, in the name of the Triple Goddess. May this be sacred earth, set apart for magic. For earth is of the Goddess, being her sacred body.* (Remember that the Goddess is not only of the Moon, but of the Earth and of the farthest stars. She is Triple Goddess of the Circle of Rebirth, the Mother of All Life.) Decorate the earth with flowers.

Now, take a wooden wand (which you should not have cut from a living tree, for no damage should be done to the woods by a witch). Ideally, you should have carved this beforehand, into the rough shape of a phallus, but a simple peeled wand will do. The wooden phallus should, of course, be an appropriate size and shape. The peeled wand, on the other hand, should be any stick of the traditional wand length (from your own fingertips to elbow) and about half an inch in diameter. You should strip this of bark, and then oil it with vegetable oil. Though not directly phallic, it retains all the symbolism of passion and the Sun's qualities. Oak is the best wood, but hazel is good too. Bless it in the name of the Lord of Day, the youthful, ardent one, the Lord of Life, the God of the greenwood. Pass the wand swiftly through the candle flame, the Bel fire, so that it becomes magically imbued, 'charged' with power. Place the wand upon the earth, saying, as you hold it there,

As the wand is to the earth,
so the male is to the female
and the Sun to our blossoming world.
Joined, they bring happiness.
May the God of Life give —— [Name something you want,
for example, *peace on Earth.*]
May the Goddess bring it forth.

Sit quietly for a while, and picture the blossoming of what you have desired in life. You will not, of course, have now brought about peace on Earth all on your own. But neither will you have been ineffective. The spells and invocations of many witches, all working on themes like these, must eventually bear fruit, because life is on the side of peace. Leave the earth and wand upon, or in front of, the altar.

Walk deosil (clockwise) three times around the circle, then spiral into the centre. Go evenly, with grace, and meditatively. Sit beside the candle flame, allowing yourself to feel peaceful. Gaze at the flame.

The next bit is different, depending on whether you are a man or a woman. Tessa, now imagine (visualize) a red rosebud in your womb. Always, your womb is the source of your creative power, whether you are pregnant with a child, an idea, a work of art or an intention. Close your eyes. Picture the light from the candle streaming into your womb, so that the rosebud blooms, unfolds. Hold this for a while, feeling the scent and silkiness, the freshness and the colour of this fully open rose within you. Feel the strength and power of your own fully blossomed capabilities. Say,

> I am woman,
> strong to conceive and to create,
> to give birth and to tend.
> As I am daughter of the Goddess,
> and blessed by the God, may I ——
>> [Here, name what you wish to bring forth in life, the form you want your creativity to take. For example, *bring healing to others* or *write my book, as I have planned* or whatever matters to you.]

Feel the strength and creative force within your womb, the centre of your being. See the power being channelled, as you have just described. Open your eyes. Always, the rose is within you.

Glyn, you should visualize a bright flame. This burns within your sexual centre, a point at the base of the stomach, just

65

above the pubic hairline. It is your own male strength and energy, which may rise through your body to be released as giving, fertilizing power, in any form, or may be the potency which impregnates, creating a physical child. It is the force which blesses and bestows, a healing and creative energy, like the shining Sun. Visualize also that you are sitting in a garden and that a rose tree is in front of you, the roses in bud. (If you prefer, it could be eglantine, the wild rose tree, in a wood.) Say,

> *I am man,*
> *and in my passion is beauty,*
> *in my warmth is life.*
> *As I am son of the Goddess,*
> *and blessed by the God,*
> *I offer my strength and vitality to——*
>> [Here name the area of life, the place, activity or the commitment you choose.]

Visualize the light streaming from you to a rose, upon the bush, so that it unfolds, blooms. Your flame is lowered by this effort. Much has gone out of you, the flame sinks down. Wait and watch, until a pink light streams from the rose towards your body. At its touch, just above the pubic hairline, the flame resurges. It burns higher and stronger than before. Open your eyes. The flame is always within you, giving itself in the ways you choose, and then rekindling.

After this, both of you should sit quietly for a moment. It would be a mistake to get up quickly. When you are ready, you can rise and jump the candle flame, making a wish.

That's the Beltane Rite for a solitary witch; or one way of doing it. It is a time of pleasure and also of mystery. Hawthorn; the white deer being hunted; the love chase; the blossoming of flowers and the greenwood – they all play a part. Be happy in your blossoming and may your summer bring fulfilment.

Blessed be,
Rae

66

30th May 1987

Dear Tessa and Glyn,

I want to write about the religious and historical basis of witchcraft and Paganism. Too many things about witchcraft would be unclear to you, without this knowledge.

People often write and talk as though witchcraft and Paganism were the same thing. They are not. A witch is correctly called a Pagan, on account of his or her religious and spiritual beliefs, but a Pagan is not invariably a witch. There are many kinds of Pagan.

Paganism is the oldest religion. It goes as far back as our cave-dwelling days. Cave paintings and carvings of both the Horned God and Mother Goddess have been found. The oldest of these are the bird-headed Goddess figurines, conveying the message of transcendence through sexuality. That grasp of the sacredness of sexuality which is the keynote of Goddess worship. These, together with archaeological remains, show the sophistication of prehistoric beliefs. But there were no multitudinous pantheons of gods and goddesses, as in the Greek and Roman Paganism of classical times. Simply the one Goddess, in the very earliest times, and then the one Horned God, her consort.

Neolithic tribal shamans, whether men or women, were the forerunners of the modern witch. They celebrated and they ritualized the changing phases of the Moon and Sun. And they practised nature magic, to obtain success in hunting for the people. They healed the sick and obtained the psychic guidance which they (and the tribe) needed, by trancework and divination. They were wisemen and wisewomen for the community. In the earliest days, the priestesses, wisewomen, would have held the highest authority, for the culture was matriarchal.

Increasingly, Pagan cults tended towards an organized form and a hierarchical structure beyond that of the local community or tribe, thus representing the official spiritual beliefs of a kingdom or group of clans. Paganism in general also tended, even before the advent of Christianity and the other god-centred religions, to become increasingly patriarchal. Witchcraft has remained a Goddess religion and therefore a personal, non-hierarchical concern, rather than an official state religion. Historically, it has been a favoured cult among oppressed peoples, because it grants spiritual autonomy to all its followers and because it puts magical power into the hands of those from whom all other kinds of power have been taken away, along with their hope and self-esteem. The Goddess and God of witchcraft are accessible, visible in the Moon and the trees, the sunlight and the rivers. They offer the magical ability to heal and soothe and to resolve problems, in their names. This religion, then, finds its roots in prehistoric beliefs; and often those beliefs were preserved by a scattered, isolated peasantry.

Archetypally, the witch has been and remains on the fringe of the fringe, outside even the outsiders. Our affinities are with, for example, the pre-Celtic inhabitants of the British Isles. These mound-dwelling, matriarchally based, Goddess-worshipping people, to whom magic was life, were long ago pushed out of the mainstream of civilization, geographically and culturally. Nowadays, they have no physical domain at all. But their blood (the so-called fairy blood) runs in the veins of some.

Throughout history, the witches have pitched their camp in any and every culture. Within, but never quite of that culture (or not since neolithic times), they have played a strange role, being sometimes scapegoated, sometimes persecuted, and often sought after as helper, healer or comforter. Through the witch, a person finds a link with an elven world; that is, with a magical reality both feared and desired. We have often had to carry the projection of other people's violent urges, sexually or psychically – and some 'witches' have indeed been suitable candidates for this role, for nature magic can be misused, like any other power.

I should like to see all humanity return to the witches' law of 'Harm none' and to the Pagan reverence for the Earth. But I do not believe we can ever institutionalize or formalize the cult of the witches. It would not then be witchcraft. However, I do believe that the time is now ripe for a return to our Pagan roots (?routes), a large-scale return. I see no reason why large numbers of people shouldn't worship the Goddess and the God and celebrate the seasons, in the ways I have been describing. But if there *were* lots of us, perhaps we should no longer be called witches (unless we showed particular aptitude as spell-casters), being no longer archetypally strange. Perhaps then we should be simply Pagans, along with all the other modern Pagans, whose worship and work may employ different techniques from ours, but which have the same or a similar basis and long-term goals. There is no reason why many should not celebrate alone or in their own families and localities; or practise uncomplicated nature magic. (Hedge Pagans?)

That is a dream. But I have a further dream that goes beyond that. It is that one day we shall, as in the earliest human tribes, have no need for priests or priestesses of any kind; nor for witches, since we shall all live in harmony with the Earth, all in communion with the Goddess and the God, living intuitively, magically. When that day comes, we shall no longer despise the feminine values, nor practise dominance, nor accept hierarchies, nor see ourselves as at all separate from the web of life. But *unlike* our ancestors, in their earliest states of innocence, we shall revere the male principle as well as the female. We shall value and worship the God as well as the Goddess, focusing on neither one to the exclusion of the other. We shall have gone on a long and difficult journey. And we shall (as at this time, particularly) have been in danger of losing our way (and maybe our world) through human stupidity and evil, and by the densest application of patriarchal values. But the world of my dream is where I hope that we are going: a world of reconciliation.

Meanwhile, as witches, we can work magically to help bring that day about. But we have one foot in fairyland and the other in the places where poor people live. We are outsiders.

Well, this is the beginning of an answer to your question, 'What is a witch?' The question was most welcome, because these letters are a process of discovery for me too. I am finding out what I believe.

In justice to other forms of modern Paganism, I would like to tell you more about them, as well as about witchcraft. But I can't. I can only tell you about what I know – about what I am. I do know that they are all new acorns from the old tree, now growing into new trees. They are a fresh religious impetus. And all, if they are worthy of the name of Paganism, seek a healing for the Earth and a return to the natural laws, to an ecological balance.

Blessed be,
Rae

New Green
Avonford

16th June 1987

Dear Tessa and Glyn,
    Rather late, as usual, this letter.
    How shall I begin about the summer solstice? The Sun is at his height, that much is clear (in spite of all the rain and the unseasonable cold: that Beltane promise of warmth didn't last long!). From now on, in terms of the cycle of the year, things will change. In the Craft, we say that the change is *because* of the culmination. Now the Sun King has known complete love with the Queen of Summer. It is because of this fulfilment that he changes his direction. Inspired by love, he begins a new quest, setting sail for the Isle of Rebirth. Thus, the Sun God will wane in the outer world, as he gains strength in inner realms, as Lord of Night.
    At the summer solstice we can celebrate all this and align ourselves with the change. Because the new adventure of the Sun King is a hero's quest, we conclude the rite by calling upon the hero/heroine in ourselves. And we call upon the Sun God to bless all the land, and to put to flight destructive forces.
    It should go without saying that a witch's heroism isn't about wielding weapons or conquering, but a matter of finding the courage to heal and transform. In the face of societal pressures to keep quiet and to acquiesce about oppression, environmental damage, industrial pollution and the continuance of nuclear stockpiling, it is also heroic to protest, politically, on behalf of Mother Earth.
    The hero's quest is vitally concerned with self-exploration, with inner development and a facing of one's own inner demons, for a full self-knowledge. The Sun God transforms the destructive forces with the light of truth.
    The summer solstice is a joyful time and celebration is itself magical. The Goddess gives us true fulfilment if we are open to her. In receiving her gift we, like the Sun, are changed and

71

filled with the power to bless. The summer solstice is the time in all the year when we are nearest to the 'Holy Grail', the cup of happiness given by the Goddess. (This is the true meaning of the Grail. It is far older than that in the Christianized Arthurian legends.)

In nature, the year has reached a peak. The leaves are out on all the trees, gardens are full of flowers and, in the fields, the crops are well established. It is a time for the enjoyment of what one has. The rite for a solitary witch takes account of all these themes.

Cast your circle and invoke both Goddess and God. A cauldron, bowl of wine or fruit juice should be at the centre of your circle.

This is my summer solstice poem for this year. You could read it aloud, or read something of your own.

Light of the Solstice Sun is seen
upon the water,
far upon the sea, fire and water, reconciled.
The Sun sets sail for what his love has shown him,
sets sail for her Otherworld.
We, too, are setting a new course,
for the Queen of Summer brings
the cup of happiness,
cup of the sweetness of desire fulfilled.
Bless us, O Queen of Summer, and bless all living creatures.
Now the peak has been reached, the change
shall be made.
Now the sails of the bright Sun are unfurled.

Dance deosil with joy and freedom. Chant *She brings the cup of happiness,/the cup of the wine of life.*

Earth the power of your dance and chanting into the cauldron. Do this by directing the gold cone into the cauldron's contents as usual. Fill your chalice with the wine or fruit juice. Say, *I drink of fulfilment.* Drink slowly and meditatively. Look into the cup from time to time. You may see visions. Feel the changes in mind, body, soul and spirit

that result from this. Give thanks to the Goddess.

Take two unlit candles from beside the altar and place one each side of the cauldron, about three feet apart on a line running east to west. Light the candles, saying, *Let the midsummer fires shine forth*. As you light them, imagine all those other midsummer fires, past and present.

Twin bonfires are a tradition at midsummer. It may be because the Sun has a dual nature, a waxing and waning side. This is often represented in mythology by rival friends or brothers. The Sun waxes in strength and vitality from winter to summer solstice. This is the first brother, strong in the outer world. In the second half of the year the other brother has ascendancy. As his physical strength wanes, he gains in the inner realms, becoming finally 'the Sun at Midnight' or 'Lord of Shadows', the Wise One. Taken together, these two make up the full being of the Sun. They are one and the same God.

Go and sit at the south quarter, the area of passion and of

change. Face in towards the twin candles and the cauldron, sitting comfortably, perhaps cross-legged. Think about what is currently bringing fulfilment to you, in your life. Is it music? Making love? Going into the countryside to be alone? Books? Your garden? If there are many things, think about them all. Think especially about any vision of fulfilment which you may just have had while drinking the wine. It is the Sun God's fate, and yours also, to be changed by a fulfilment. Let us say that, for one of you, the greatest current fulfilment is learning about the Craft, studying to become a witch. For the other, it is the new relationship. You are in love. Each of you should think about this (or whatever it may be), feeling the energy of your passion flaming up and impelling you to make changes. Visualize these changes. See them as though they have already happened. See your life as it would be afterwards. Think about the steps you must take to bring this into being; or better, see if you can perceive, intuitively, what you must do. Silently, make your pledges to the Goddess about these steps. Now take another candle (which should have been placed ready at the south quarter). Light it from the midsummer fire on the western side of the cauldron. Before you light it, hold it for a while, imbuing it with power, consecrating it. For added magical effect, anoint it with oil of rosemary, or rub it with the fresh leaves. Rosemary is a herb sacred to the Sun, and also has connections with the sea. It is said to bring a safe voyage. As you touch your candle to the flame, say, *As this candle burns, so may the change be made. May I ——* [list all the steps you mean to take].

Now take the candle deosil from the south quarter (summer) through the west (autumn) to the north (winter). Place it upon the altar. Leave it to burn all the way down. You may move it, when the rite ends, but do not extinguish it.

Now rest awhile, enjoying the candle-light. Drink more wine, if you want to. Then take a wand of wood and consecrate it. Bless it in the names of the Triple Goddess and the Horned God, dedicating it to magic. Pass it swiftly through or touch it to the incense, candle flame, water and stone (or pentacle) upon your altar.

Stand with your back to the altar, facing south, and raise the wand high in the air. You are about to invoke for protection and blessing upon the land, to call down the blessing of the Sun. Simple invocations are the most powerful. You may be able to speak spontaneously, or you may feel more confident if you have planned and learned what you want to say beforehand. It could be something like this:

I call upon the power of the bright Sun King,
as he makes his journey to the Otherworld.
As he draws away, may he still
shine in blessing, upon this land,
bringing peace and plenty.
And I call upon him now, to vanquish all —— [for
example, *oppression*].
May this be put to flight in his name.

Wave the wand. Continue around the circle, waving the wand at each quarter, saying, *Peace and plenty. All [oppression] vanquished from the four quarters of this land.*

Sit quietly for a while after this. It is then time for communion, after which the rite is ended.

Enjoy yourselves. Celebrate in style!

Bright and blessed be,
Rae

75

New Green
Avonford

3rd July 1987

Dear Tessa and Glyn,

I want to answer Glyn's question, 'Why does witchcraft always have to take place formally, within a circle? Surely, we could worship and work magic anywhere, wherever we are?'

The short answer is, We generally work inside a clearly defined, protected, sacred space because it's easier that way. The heightened consciousness necessary for communion and spell-casting is more easily attained 'between the worlds'. The Goddess and the God are all around us to be communed with, it is true. Most especially in nature, in a wood or garden, in a field or hedgerow, they are everywhere to be seen. But the magical awareness that we reach within the circle can't be lived through every mundane moment. Just as it would be hard to compose music beside a pneumatic drill, it can be very difficult to attain the clarity and inner focus needed for an invocation in the psychic atmosphere of today's everyday world. The magic circle allows the existence of a different, more sacred atmosphere, and the build-up of magical power.

Having told you that witchcraft can't easily be practised anywhere and everywhere, and having told you why, I am now going to tell you that people do do it, nevertheless, and that you can too. If a friend has just been admitted to hospital and you have been phoned and informed that there is to be an emergency operation, you aren't going to wait for the next suitable phase of the Moon, or even to cast a full circle. You are just going to cast your spell for healing, right then and there. And this is how you do it.

Sit in the most peaceful and comfortable place that you can find, and close your eyes. Now visualize yourself surrounded by a blue sphere of light. Remember that whatever you can imagine *has* an actual existence, astrally: it is, on the inner planes, really there. Call upon the Guardian Spirits of the four directions to aid and protect you. Picture the appropriate

76

offering, as you invoke the protection of each one, so that you are surrounded not only by blue light, but also by incense at the east, a candle at the south, a bowl of water at the west and a pentacle or dish of earth at the north. There is no need to worry that these things will disappear; they will remain as long as you desire them, as will the Guardian Spirits; just as the parts of a room that are behind you go on being there, even when you aren't looking.

Now you are 'between the worlds', in a light trance. Take time over this: it can't be hurried. You have turned inwards, into the astral world; down, in, through. Here, there is infinite possibility, unending distance, just as there is in outer space, in the universe. Within this realm, you have defined an area. Invoke the presence of the Goddess and the God, just as though you were in a formally cast circle. Ask for their assistance. Talk to them about your magical intention. Deep within yourself, utter the words that you want to say. There is no need for special language. Just offer to them your thoughts and your feelings. Place the outcome of your magic in their hands.

Now open your eyes and cast your spell. It may be, perhaps, that you wish to light a candle to the healing of your friend. First, consecrate the candle. As you light it, say, *As this flame burns may the flame of life burn bright in* —— [the friend's name] *carrying her through the time of danger. As the candle lowers, so may her vitality arise. The longer that it burns, the more healed may she be, by the power of the Guardian Spirits and in the names of the Triple Goddess and her consort, Lord of Day and Night.* The above is just an example of words to accompany a candle spell for healing. In practice, you will find that you know what to say at the time, and that you rarely use the same formula more than once.

You might follow this by consecrating a small bottle of essential oil of lavender or sandalwood, both healing oils, to be given as a magical gift for your friend's complete recovery.

Spells can be impromptu, and may not always be about healing. And you may have to use whatever materials are to hand. Once, when I was in a city, I bought a greetings card and consecrated it in a café to magic. It was the whole physical means and medium of my spell. On the front, it bore a picture of a house. The spell was to obtain a new home. I posted it to myself and Cole. It was soon successful.

Before returning to the world, the outer world, you should again close your eyes. Thank the Goddess and the God and the Guardian Spirits, as though ending a formal rite within a circle. Leave the blue sphere of light around yourself and visualize a protective pentacle, just above your head, to remain there as long as you may need it. Now open your eyes and go about your other activities.

I once saw a successful spell cast for the healing of a friend's disease, in a crowded pub. It was done using paper from an ordinary notebook, a red Biro, matches and a pub ashtray. The friend's name and the name of the illness were written in red and the paper then burnt in the ashtray, with the statement that, as it burnt, so should the illness be burned out of her and die. The friend did recover, although it had not been expected that she would. She is still fit and well, eight years later.

Witchcraft can be practised anywhere, though the witch who cast this spell was experienced. His abilities to concentrate, visualize, invoke and focus an intent were well honed and well developed – and had doubtless become so through many years of practice inside the circle, and in deep trancework in more peaceful environments.

I do not advise either of you to do spells in crowded places, not just at first. Such magic can go wrong because, if you work spontaneously within a jarring atmosphere, you may lack adequate perception about how, or indeed whether, a spell should be cast. And your own psychic balance may be disturbed. Use discretion and humility. Paradoxically, 'pub spells' done in the most uncomplicated manner, are for the most experienced. You could get your fingers burned in more ways than one!

It is a strange fact of life that the more unskilled we are, magically, the more magical paraphernalia we need to be effective. Even the very skilled are *more* effective with all their specialized magical tools and equipment – athame, robe, wand, cauldron, and so on. These things have a beauty and an ancient symbolic meaning. They also become highly charged with power and meaning from long use, so that just to touch them is already to be halfway 'between the worlds'.

Sometimes, it takes all our humility to admit how much we need these tools, a formal ritual and a formally marked-out space: somewhere sacred, set apart. But that is how it is, in the world of today.

Bright and blessed be,
Rae

New Green
Avonford

22nd July 1987

Dear Tessa and Glyn,

Now we approach the Festival of the First Fruits. Its Celtic name Lughnasadh means 'mourning for Lugh', while the Saxon name of Lammas means 'loaf-mass'. Since Lugh was an ancient name for the Sun God, these two titles sum up much of the festival's meaning. Summer is on the wane, the Sun's strength dwindles and we mourn his passing. This is a wake, as well as a celebration. But there is also a birth, the tender beginnings of harvest. The Sun's power has 'gone into the corn'. Soon this will be cut down, and so he will be reborn, 'the Bread of Life'. In this can be seen the underlying reasons for the theme of sacrifice.

As I said in an earlier letter, blood was actually spilt at Lammas in the past, when the man-who-stood-in-for-the-God was ritually sacrificed to ensure a good harvest. This was at a time when the pure essence of Pagan worship had been corrupted, and the people's understanding had become crude. What caused the corruption? Historically, it seems to have been the rise of patriarchy. Philosophically, I believe it has to do with the nature of manifest life. Certainly, everything goes through this same cycle of pure seed beginning, followed by established growth, corruption and decay, then death and eventual rebirth (often in a wiser or more integrated form).

Back to this year's Lammas Rite. At the Festival of the First Fruits we assess the coming harvest, seeing the very first signs, the first fruits. And we look to see what acts or sacrifices can alleviate any damage or avert any loss of crops.

The Goddess is giving birth now, and we celebrate this birth, the fruits of field and orchard, garden and hedgerow. At the same time, the God's strength wanes, dies and is reborn. Like any man in sexual union, his strength is given to her. For the seed leaves a man's body and along with it goes life energy. He revives to make love again, sooner or later.

But the energy he has given can help to create a child. She takes it and transforms it, and then a child is born. This is the inner meaning of Lammas. We celebrate the life energy that the God has given, as well as all the creation that the Goddess is bringing forth.

A solitary witch might begin Lammas with a walk in the country. I know that you two both have access to this. For those who don't, there are parks, back gardens, canal paths and 'waste' land. Look for the first fruits of harvest. Are there blackberries on bushes? If you are in the countryside, how does the corn look? Is it golden and tall or still green and unripe? How do these things compare with your life? If you set yourself to learn something back at Candlemas, are you making progress? If you are a craftsperson, are you satisfied with your techniques? In your business or profession, are you making any headway? In the cycle of this year's life, and in longer cycles, are there fruits?

Bring back a hedgerow fruit to place upon the altar.

On the night of Lammas, cast your circle and invoke the Lady and the Lord. Through them, the harvest time has come round again. Give thanks for the first signs of harvest in your life, as well as in the fields. For the two go hand in hand, and how can we be fruitful if the Earth is not?

When you feel ready to raise some power, dance deosil around an unlit candle, in the cauldron, at the centre of your circle. Your chant could be like this:

For Sun we mourn
as he shall wane.
The crops remain.

Through kern and corn,
the harvest born,
shall life return.

Our Mother Earth
now brings to birth
the life poured forth
in light and warmth.

81

Alternatively, you can chant some wild and complex poem of your own making. Use your wand to direct the power into the candle. As you light it, say *Now may the light shine forth, and may the harvest ripen. For we live by the land, and only by her health and fruitfulness can we be rich in health and fruitfulness. Sun shine in strength and brilliance. Sun pour out blessings on the land. I light this candle to the Sun.*

You should have with you a small bowl of vegetable oil. Sunflower is suitable, but whatever it is, it should be the best-quality oil that you can buy. It represents an offering. The bowl should be plain pottery or wood. Consecrate the oil, setting it aside for magic. Then pass the bowl swiftly through the Lammas flame. Now, sitting cross-legged beside the cauldron, gaze into the oil. All oil has connections, symbolic and practical, with fire, heat, flames, and thus with the Sun. And the Sun gives strength and brightness to the Goddess-as-Mother-Earth. Say aloud, *Now as the Sun pours out his strength upon the Earth, that the crops may ripen, and that the harvest may be great, I too offer my strength to the Goddess, to Mother Earth. I bring —— [for example, *my intention to protect the Earth from further harm, where and when I can*].

Make any pledge that you can make sincerely, and breath it into the oil. Visualize the energy you will give to the fulfilling of this promise. See it as a gold stream carried on your breath, that then merges with the oil, and carries the magical 'charge' of your offering.

Then take the oil deosil around the circle to the altar. Touch it to your stone or pentacle, thus 'giving it to the Earth'. Leave the bowl on the altar and return to sit silently beside the cauldron, until you are ready for the next part of the rite. Think about your promise; see yourself carrying it out; and see the fruitful consequences. (After the rite is ended, pour the oil onto the earth in your garden.)

Now take from the altar the hedgerow or garden fruit, representing first fruits of a harvest in your life, a symbolic indication of your hopes. If you were a painter, for example, your hope might be to produce many good pictures. If you

were a fruit farmer, then it might literally be a rich harvest of fruit. But Lammas is also a good time to think about any long-term harvest that you hope for in your life. Do you see any first fruits of this? If not, do your hopes need reassessing? Are they unrealistic or are they too pedestrian? Do you underestimate yourself, or life?

Take the fruit deosil around the circle and then sit beside the cauldron. Think about and visualize the harvest. What qualities and what creation do you hope for? What 'results' would you like your life to have? Children? Successful spells for the healing of Earth? Wisdom? Love? The making of music? Seen from this perspective, much of what human beings worry about is revealed as surprisingly irrelevant. For the Lammas meditation measures everyday concerns against a long-term ideal.

Name out loud the harvest that you hope for, and place the fruit in the cauldron, by the candle.

There is probably some reason why you fear that the harvest will not materialize, after all. Most of us do fear that we will fail, somehow or other. For example, a person may want to paint, but may have no confidence in her own talent; or she may feel guilty, since time spent painting is time not spent in nurturing other people.

Take your athame in one hand, and with the other remove the candle in its holder from the cauldron. Gently inscribe the words (or symbolic picture) summing up your obstacle, on the candle stem. Use the point of your athame. It need not be clearly etched. The intention is what matters.

Say, *As the candle burns and the word* [or *picture*] *is gone, so may my* —— [for example, *guilt*] *be gone. May it be transformed, as wax becomes a flame, an illumination.*

Wipe the point of your athame on a cloth, to remove any wax.

Now celebrate the harvest which is to come. Play music, dance or write a poem, sing or make something or draw a picture. Whatever you do, it should be enjoyable. Be aware that what you do in fun and celebration in the circle will enhance your creativity in life. Burial and birth and bread, these are the themes of Lammas, but it is not a sombre time. It is a thankful time. The first fruits are there to be enjoyed and to encourage hope. They are a sign of what will be, at the main harvest.

The Lammas communion is especially sacred. Take a loaf of bread (which preferably should be home-baked, but any wholemeal loaf will do). This is, or will become, the Bread of Life, that which arises from the Sun's sacrifice. It is, essentially, the Sun's life-energy, reborn as bread.

Pass the loaf through the candle flame, then carry it round the circle deosil, holding it high at each quarter, and finally holding it high above the altar. Say a prayer of consecration and invocation, something like this: *Now the Sun fades and the corn will be cut down, the God dies. He is life itself and his spirit passes into the corn and into all the crops and every kind of harvest. Changed, he is reborn, for life cannot ever finally die.*

Cut a slice of bread with your athame. Before eating it, say,

I, priestess [priest] and Witch, eat of the Bread of Life on

behalf of all people, that all may be fed. This is the Bread of Immortality. Though everything must die, I know that by this nourishment we share rebirth. From moment to moment, year to year and life to life, we die and are reborn, transformed. We are not separate nor ever, finally, alone. For this, the Bread of Life, is the Bread of Communion

Keep the rest of the bread to share with family and friends.

Now consecrate and drink the wine.

When you are ready, thank the Goddess and God for their blessing on your rite, and thank the Guardian Spirits, bidding them, *Hale and farewell*. Open the circle. Wise and blessed be. Eat of the Bread of Life with happiness.

Bright blessings,
Rae

New Green
Avonford

26th August 1987

Dear Tessa and Glyn,

These rites which I send you are ideas and suggestions, nothing more. Once you have grasped the basic principles of any ritual, you can create your own. In witchcraft, there is no dogma, no set liturgy. Instead, there are traditions. Once you have understood them, it is up to you. The Craft will live through you, and through what you bring to it. And it is these traditions, these eternal themes, which I want to convey. You will find them referred to by other writers on the Craft, and sometimes you will see them in mythology and folklore. So read widely and learn everything you can on the subject of witchcraft and Paganism. Learn, as well, the related disciplines of divination, trancework, natural philosophy, herb magic, the properties of plants and trees and all countryside lore. You will then develop your own feelings about, for example, the spring equinox and how it should be celebrated. In time, you will develop your own style. This is the strength of witchcraft. Its roots are in the oldest religion and yet it is created anew, by each individual witch, every time it is practised.

Witches of the Gardnerian and Alexandrian school (that is, the modern mainstream of British witchcraft) have certain fixed and definitive forms for many of their rites. Yet the structure and definition are not so final that they do not permit a creative improvisation and alteration. This is as it should be, for a religion which had crystallized would be dead. There must always be room for change.

These 'mainstream' rites are based on handed-down material expanded and developed by Gerald Gardner, a precursor of the first wave of the Pagan revival. Following the repeal of the Witchcraft Act, in 1951, he was able to make public certain old teachings which became the basis of much modern witchcraft. His followers are called Gardnerians.

Alexandrian witches work in a manner initiated by a couple, Alex and Maxine Sanders, and constructed on the foundation of Gardnerian ritual, but with amendments. Alexandrian rites and beliefs have been extensively described by Pagan writers, Janet and Stewart Farrar. Their books and those of Gerald Gardner, and of his original High Priestess Doreen Valiente, who wrote or adapted many passages in Gardner's final Book of Shadows, producing a coherent and consistent whole, give a comprehensive introduction to the ideals and practices of 'Wicca' (modern witchcraft). They are all worthwhile reading for any apprentice witch, in spite of the fact that they teach mostly about the structure of ritual for covens.

The Gardnerian rituals and teachings are authentically traditional. The basics were handed on to Gardner by the New Forest coven which had initiated him. Nevertheless, there is no such thing as holy writ or law in witchcraft. The whole Pagan world owes an immense debt to Gardner and to Doreen Valiente for the richness and the inspiration of their Book of Shadows, and for the feeling of heritage which it gives to all witches, even to those like us, who may draw upon it but work in other ways. However, it is not the last word.

There are many schools of witchcraft in existence, many organized forms of teaching, which are increasingly available. The followers of each one, in the past, would have been happy to tell you that theirs was the best, or even the Only True Way to become a real witch. Some would still do so now. Don't listen to them.

This letter is to say, Don't take anyone's word as the last, least of all mine. Listen to everybody, and then let yourself be guided into doing things in your own way.

Blessings on your search for knowledge. May it lead you to yourself.

Perhaps you are wondering about my story, about how I came to be a witch? Was I initiated, and by whom? But if self-initiated, at whose suggestion and because of whose teachings?

Well, I was once associated with an Alexandrian coven, though not fully initiated. I have never been through full initiation into any coven, and I would not wish to. The Alexandrians whom I knew were kind and informative but I felt that their way was not for me. It was not what I had meant, when I first knew that I was going to become a witch. On the advice and with the help of a Gardnerian High Priest, a friend, I broke all links with them and returned to the solitary path of Self-Initiation which I had initially chosen. Since then, I have been helped by many people, either through their books or through conversation. The work of Marian Green, teacher of village witchcraft, has been a big influence. So have Starhawk's books. And so have the beliefs and the occult fiction of my life-partner, Cole. And then there is Rowena, Gardnerian priestess, whose aspirations and life direction have taken her from a coven and into the role of solitary wisewoman. Her words have often helped me to become clear about my own direction. Weaving through all this and leading to or identifying the next strand, there has always been inner guidance.

Nowadays, it sounds corny to declare 'I was guided' to this, that or the other person, book or idea. However, I was. Without these inner contacts, all ideas are arid intellectual concepts, lacking real resonance for the person who finds them. And, as any true witch will tell you, it is this inner experience, this access to psychic reality behind the concepts and the ritual observances, that makes a witch.

So if a witch is what you truly are, you will develop these contacts. Others will help you to do so. That is my own aim, to put you in touch with Pagan inner realms. For those who have been on this path before, it need not take much to achieve this.

Wise and blessed be,
Rae

New Green
Avonford

15th September 1987

Dear Tessa and Glyn,

The time of the harvest is almost here, time of the weighing-up of both gains and losses. Concurrently, the Sun is about to enter the sign of the scales, Libra. So balancing is a strong theme, as well as thanksgiving. Day and night will be equal, as at the spring equinox, but after this festival, the dark gains. The days grow shorter, right through to the winter solstice.

This is the autumn equinox. It is Harvest Festival, the time to celebrate and give thanks, and to throw out and clear away unwanted things, the chaff and rubbish. A double-sided festival, even double-edged.

The universal symbol for reincarnation, the double spiral, is the special symbol for this time of year. The meaning of this is that a breathing out is always followed (balanced) by an indrawn breath, as sleep is followed by awakening and death is followed by rebirth. So the double spiral brings a message as we wind in towards the still point, or darkest night, the winter solstice. You may wonder from where the double spiral derives? Well, spirals have been used symbolically in many lands and at all times, right from the Stone Age. They are carved onto standing stones and burial chambers. The double spiral shows both a going-in and a returning, hence rebirth. Interestingly, it is also the shape of the DNA. But that could not have been known in the past, except perhaps intuitively. It seems to be an underlying pattern of all life. Researchers into geodetic force have discovered the spiral's associations with electrical energy created by blind springs and underground streams.

The Goddess is Lady of Abundance. Her cauldron, cornucopia, produces all good things, an abundance of blessings. The God is Lord of Harvest. Their union is fruitful and has made all things on Earth.

89

You could begin an autumn-equinox rite by decorating room and altar with autumn flowers and fruits. Cast the circle and invoke the Lady and the Lord of All Abundance.

An unlit candle should be in the cauldron, at the centre. Round the candle's base should be ears of corn. Light the candle, saying:

Welcome now to the autumn equinox, time of the double spiral, of the winding-in upon the thread of fate, towards the still point in the darkness, where there is rebirth of light and life. Thus, all must journey through the realm of winter. And the harvest, the grain that has been reaped, sustains us through the winter season, holding seeds that shall be planted in spring. For the circle of life is unbroken.
I light this candle to the waning Sun.

90

Walk widdershins (anticlockwise) around the cauldron seven times. Then spiral in towards the centre. Kneel or sit cross-legged beside the cauldron. Take from it the ears of corn, saying,

> *Times of waning bring a harvest.*
> *Towards endings, there are fruits.*
> *As we journey through winter, realm of death,*
> *the fruits of life sustain us*
> *and contain the seeds*
> *of new life. This mystery is seen,*
> *is everywhere revealed,*
> *and yet is sealed*
> *in silence and in darkness.*

Gaze at the corn. Close your eyes and picture it as the essence of Sun and Earth, containing the new life. Here, in the harvest, are the seeds of the next cycle. How does this reveal the mysteries? Ask the Goddess to show you now, if she will. You may see visions of cycles, circles, or of the dark journey to the Underworld and back again, a labyrinthine journey. Ask to understand the purpose behind this, or within it, the true purpose of creation. If you are blessed with understanding, this is an inner harvest. Give thanks for anything you see, and open your eyes. Carrying the corn, spiral out deosil, and walk seven times around the circle.

Place the ears of corn upon the altar. Later, they can be tied with a red ribbon and hung throughout winter somewhere in the house.

Standing before the altar, say:

> *I celebrate the gain, the fruits,*
> *and all of the Earth's abundance,*
> *dancing the outgoing*
> *and the incoming spiral.*
> *Every end is followed by beginning.*

Pause for a moment, then continue:

> *The incoming flow*
> *in seeds that shall grow*
> *lies hidden till spring.*
> *The unbroken ring of rebirth.*
> *The harvest sustain,*
> *till spring comes again.*
> *Season of gain.*
> *The seeds shall remain!*

Repeat the last two lines as a chant. Dance deosil, joyfully, building creative power, a dance of life. (You should not be wearing any swirling robes or cloaks for this, because of the naked flame.) Earth the energy into three cords or ribbons, which you will have placed inside the cauldron. Plait the cords, in a length long enough to be worn as a necklace. Then the ends should be fastened, creating a circle.

As you plait, visualize that you are weaving in the harvest richness of this year, anything and everything that gives hope for life on Earth. Name, as you weave, the victories, even small and local ones, on environmental issues; any inspirational books you have read; any changes of public opinion about exploitation of natural resources; any ending to any war; any successful creative effort by any person or group; any justice or any resolution of conflict anywhere on Earth. These are the seeds of new ways. They are stars within the Circle of Rebirth.

As you fasten the ends and complete the circle, say, *The unbroken circle. Life shall never die.*

Hold the necklace high above the altar, then put it on. Later, it should be kept in some safe place until the spring equinox, when it may be buried and thus magically returned to Earth, for Earth's continued being.

Sit quietly for a while and think about the spell you have cast. Visualize the Earth healed. See life continuing.

When you are ready, return to the altar and give thanks to

the Goddess and the God for your personal harvest, for what you have reaped in your own life. Place an offering – perhaps a poem or picture or something you have made – upon the altar. Next, visit each of the four quarters, just as you did at the spring equinox. This time, bring an offering to each quarter, in thanks.

At the east quarter, meditate upon your harvest of ideas, your concepts and realizations. Close your eyes and think of all the new ideas you have received in the last year. Give thanks to the Guardian Spirits of Air, and then place a handful of incense on some smouldering charcoal, or light some more joss, in offering.

At the south, close your eyes and think about any improvements in health and vitality, or any successes or adventures, any 'high peaks'. Give thanks for these, or for any beneficial changes, and then anoint the candle with an essential oil, in offering. Rosemary or frankincense are suitable.

At the west, meditate on your emotional fulfilment and give thanks for this, for friendships, skill in magic or experiences of enchantment and beauty. Pour a little wine or apple juice into the water, in offering.

At the north, see and give thanks for the manifest blessings which you have harvested, the physical results of work done in the home or the garden, artistically, creatively, or in your job. Make an offering of bread and leave it on the altar by your stone, or on top of the dish of earth, or pentacle.

At the centre of your circle, by the cauldron, visualize the way in which the elements of your life interweave to create the whole essence of your being. Give thanks for any way in which you see new integration in yourself, your life. Is there any one principle or activity which seems to uphold the rest? Name it. Then take a white cord from within the cauldron. As an offering, tie in it five knots, one for each quarter and one for the centre, the still point. Tie the ends of the cord together and keep this also until the spring.

Meditate for a moment upon the loss and gain in your life. What is slipping away? This is the time to let it go, with thanks for what has been; or purposely to cast aside what you don't need, the chaff. But your harvest, for which you have just given thanks, contains the seeds of the next cycle. See the balance.

After a communion, the circle is 'open but not broken'. Then you step outside the place between the worlds, and on your way into the autumn.

Blessed be,
Rae

Dear Tessa and Glyn,

I have said that Bride Day was traditionally the time most favoured for the making of new witches. But that does not mean no other time is right. In fact, any Sabbat or Full Moon will do. Within these guidelines, the day chosen should be an individual matter. You yourself will know when you are ready. I will therefore give you the self-initiation rite now, to do at a time of your choosing.

To be a witch requires not only self-discipline in personal development, but a sense of fulfilment in your Craft which outweighs social pressures: the sideways looks and mistrust from those who know what you are, what you practise; the feeling of a barrier between you and those who don't know, because you can't tell them; the possible active discrimination; the obvious implications where friends and lovers are concerned. If you are a born witch, you will, of course, ignore these warnings, and quite rightly.

An initiation rite is customarily a death-and-rebirth sequence, symbolizing that the old life is now over and a new one has begun. It also involves a pledge or offering, a consecration and the taking of a new name. Then there is instruction in techniques or some new experience – admittance to the mysteries.

No one can make you into a witch. Nothing that happens *to* you can change you in the least, unless there is that inner change that makes the difference. In other words, the true making of a witch happens between the individual and the Goddess and Horned God. It is an inner, psychic change, dependent on willingness and suitability. Though others can help you to mark a rite of passage, in the last resort no one can mediate between you and the Gods. You are on your own, responsible for your own spirit. Can you offer yourself upon this path sincerely? If so, you will be accepted. And it will be in privacy, with no one watching over you but the Guardian Spirits.

There is more than one rite of self-initiation in existence. I am about to give you my version. As with any true resolution, if your vow or pledge has been accepted, you will know. You will feel it at the time as a profound and *perceptible* expansion of awareness.

Your new name should not be told to anyone, except to another witch. It is the symbol of your witch self, your magical persona. It should have potency, a sacred meaning for you. It could be a plant name, or that of an animal or bird. It could be the name of a place that has either personal or mystical significance for you, or both. Many witches have taken the names of characters from myth, legend or occult law. Be inventive but unpretentious. Ask for guidance if you cannot easily find it.

Prepare for the initiation with a cleansing bath. (Add salt or a handful of purifiying herbs to the water.) When you cast the circle, you should work naked or, as witches say, sky-clad. This is one rite which should be performed without clothes or jewellery. Thus, you stand before the Goddess and God without defences or any attributes of your old life. For to begin anew, you must be stripped of old ways and cast away old assumptions, habits and self-image.

Invoke the Goddess and the God, in your own words.

Cut off a small lock of your hair with your athame. Hold it high above the altar in offering. Say, *I call upon the Guardian Spirits of the elements to witness that I now offer myself to the Triple Goddess of the Circle of Rebirth and to the Horned God, as witch and priestess [priest].*

Carry the hair deosil around the circle, holding it up at each quarter. Place it upon the altar, saying, *By this token, I am theirs.* (The power of a witch is said by some to be within his or her unbound hair. If you had no hair upon your head, for reasons of age, perhaps, then body hair would do as a substitute.)

Wrap yourself in a cloak or blanket for warmth, and go deosil to the west quarter. Sit comfortably and close your eyes. Ask for guidance as you walk the sacred path. Visualize yourself walking a path through woodland. It is a little overgrown and flanked by wildflowers. There are oak, ash and hawthorn trees. It is an old path. Suddenly it goes downhill. Follow it to the mouth of a cave and go inside. There is a candle standing on a rock. By its light, you can see that the cave is clear and clean. The air is fresh. In one corner is a small pool, filled by a bubbling spring. The water flows from this pool, out through the cave entrance. The bottom is covered in sand and smooth stones. Take off your clothes and get into the pool. The water takes from you all doubt and hesitation, all fear and fetters. It washes away any bonds from your old life that could hinder your work as priestess/priest and witch. Think about the meaning of being a witch as you bathe. You may receive guidance.

Step out of the pool and leave the cave. Outside, on the ground, you will find some clothes. These are your 'witch's garb'. They are the dress of your new role. They may be robes or a cloak or a tunic and trousers. Whatever they are, first dry yourself on a rough square of cloth, and then put them on. Notice what they seem to symbolize, in terms of colour and so on, what they mean to you. Among them, you may find some special object, a staff, a piece of jewellery or something else. It is a symbol of your future life as a witch, showing something of your particular duties and skills. Take it with you and carry on along the path.

You will see a magnificent tree: strong, leafy, deep-rooted and joyous. Walk up to it, lay your forehead against the trunk and put your arms around it. Sense the sap, all the strong life of the tree. Know that you and the tree are one, being different expressions of the same life energy, both created from Air and Fire and Water and Earth. You are fellow beings, together with the stars and rocks and animals and birds and all creation. Sense the tree's spirit. It may tell you something that you need to know. Thank the tree and walk away along the path. Once again, ask the Goddess and God to guide you from now on. Ask the Guardian Spirits to assist you in your work as witch and priest/priestess.

Open your eyes. Do not get up too quickly. Remember any message or impression you have received. Then, leaving your cloak or blanket at the west quarter, go deosil to the east and then inwards to the cauldron. Take from it a small bowl containing pure vegetable oil, or essential oil of cypress, frankincense or sandalwood. Place it upon the altar. Say,

> *Tonight, I pledge myself for all time*
> *to serve and celebrate the Triple Goddess*
> *and the Horned God, as witch and priest/priestess.*
> *I set myself to walk this sacred path*
> *from this time on. I name myself* —— [recite your magical name]
> *and I call now upon the Guardian Spirits*
> *to witness my consecration.*

Anoint yourself, touching the oil with the tips of your fingers just above the pubic hairline, between the breasts, on the forehead and the crown of the head, saying, *Blessed be my body and my soul, my mind and my spirit.*

Remain before the altar in silence for a few moments, and then say, *I ask to be remade as witch and priest/priestess in perfect love and perfect trust, and with the qualities of* —— [Here list the highest qualities you can think of, whether abstract virtues such as honesty, benevolence, compassion, courage, or abilities, such as 'far-sightedness, like the hawk' or 'magical speech, like the nightingale.'].

Stay silent for a moment longer, with closed eyes. On the inner levels, you may hear voices, music, or just a long-drawn-out 'hiss' (like the sound light seems to make when it travels between the stars). You may see visions. Do not try to see or hear anything. But just let whatever happens come naturally. Then visit each of the four quarters in turn, saying, *I* —— [new name], *ask acknowledgement from the Guardian Spirits of Air (Fire, Water, Earth), as witch and priest/priestess.*

Kneel before the altar and place one hand on the crown of your head and the other beneath your feet, saying, *All between my hands belongs to the Goddess.*

You are now ready to consecrate your athame, the magical knife, first working tool of a witch. Pass the blade through the smoke of the incense and through the flame of the candle. Sprinkle it with water and touch it to your dish of earth, or pentacle. Place the knife between your two hands. Say, *I bless, consecrate and set apart this athame, by the power of Air, Fire, Water and Earth and in the names of the Triple Goddess of the Circle of Rebirth, and of the Horned God, Lord of Death who is Lord of Life. May it serve me well for magic uses, a true sacred implement of witchcraft.* Pour into it your own psychic energy. End with the traditional conclusion to any spell: *So may it be.*

From now on, charged with magic, your knife will be many times more effective in the casting of spells, whether it is used to cut a cord, to carve something or to direct and define, as when casting a circle. Replace the knife on the altar. At a future Sabbat or Full Moon, you should consecrate the altar itself, and all tools of magic, such as chalice, wand, cauldron, incense holder, candlesticks, water bowl and pentacle or stone. Use the point of your athame rather than your hands, to direct power and to render each one sacred and set apart. Thereafter, you should also consecrate materials used in a spell. (Be careful when consecrating herbs, as their subtle energies are said to be reduced by direct contact with metal. Hold the blade a little away.)

End your rite with a communion. Then make a final toast to 'the Old Ones', the Old Gods, as the Goddess and God of the witches have traditionally been known. In the traditional wording, this goes, *To the Old Ones. Merry meet and merry part and merry meet again.*

Although this toast is drunk to the Old Gods, Cole and I have always found that we also think here of those other 'old ones', the old-time initiates of our Craft, all our spiritual forebears, whether working at the dawn of time when they were venerated for their wisdom, or in secret in the times of persecution. All those other countless, unknown witches. It is as though we join with them, as we sit and drink our wine.

Open the circle. You should now, after clearing away all your magical tools, go straight to bed. Your dreams may be memorable, and could bring further guidance.

Wise and blessed be,
Rae

New Green
Avonford

21st October 1987

Dear Tessa and Glyn,

I have written a note to myself about this letter. It goes, 'Don't forget to mention "trick-or-treating".' So I'll say what I want to say about that now. Trick-or-treating, as I am sure you both know, is a new 'custom' which has come from America. It requires that children go from door to door, demanding 'treats' if they are not to play a 'trick' upon the occupants. As a matter of fact, it's well in keeping with Samhain, or Hallowe'en, the night on which it takes place. Samhain is a 'mischief night' on which sprites are expected to play tricks on humankind on behalf of the Lord of Misrule, that aspect of the Horned One who will not let us take ourselves too seriously. The Lord of Misrule also loosens things up with surprises, jokes and bizarre happenings because the boundaries dissolve at Samhain, and the worlds begin to merge. Trick-or-treating children are his emissaries perhaps.

So what can you do if you don't want your worship and spell-casting interrupted? Either begin a bit later than usual, or postpone your celebration till the next night. Personally, I can never bear to miss the special atmosphere of 31st October, so I risk the door-knocking of mischievous sprites and somehow it seems to work out.

This festival is about the year's death and therefore is the New Year, for death implies rebirth. But at this time, the death is more obvious than the intangible rebirth. Fields lie fallow, the sap has sunk down into roots and all of nature rests. There is an atmosphere of weirdness in the autumnal mists and the smoky colours of evening. This is, in fact, the Festival of the Returning Dead, as well as an acknowledgement of the end of one solar cycle. That is why it has its reputation for ghostly happenings, its bats'-wings-and-black-cloaks associations.

101

Janet and Stewart Farrar, in *Eight Sabbats for Witches*, make the following comment: 'Samhain is a time of psychic eeriness, for at the turn of the year – the old dying, the new still unborn – the Veil [is] very thin.'

The old year dissolves, it breaks down, at Samhain, and the result is a breakdown of all boundaries, including those between the living and the dead. It is therefore more possible than usual to perceive the psychic presence of those who have died before us but who are still connected, still watching over us. That is one reason for ghostly events at Hallowe'en. The living, the dead and the unborn can meet in spirit on this night, psychically communing and exchanging information. Likewise, the nature spirits walk among us, both the kindly and the more mischievous ones.

Not surprisingly, Samhain is the best night of all the year for clairvoyance and divination. Some of the visions and psychic messages are said to be sent by the Beloved Dead, that is, by the dead friends or family members with whom we are still linked by bonds of affection. Others may be a direct gift from the Goddess. All are to be taken seriously. Experience has shown Cole and I that they often provide the key to the major theme of the whole coming year, but in symbolic terms.

On this subject of the return of the Beloved Dead, there is no tradition in witchcraft which in any way justifies an attempt to 'call the dead back'. Witches believe that the dead join us freely on this night, if they are able and if they wish to. Calling them back may interfere with the stages of purification, rest and preparation for a new life, which all go through between incarnations. Any attempt to force something will probably fail anyway if it is mistimed. But if it should succeed it could disrupt a natural process and actually be harmful to the returning spirit. So at Samhain, witches ritualize a welcome to the Beloved Dead, and then simply wait. If a loving spirit should desire to come back, they will be recognized. If not, we can remember them with love and then accept their absence.

By the way, and in case you are wondering, I have never

heard of a witch being troubled by the return of an unloving spirit at Samhain. I think this may be because the psychic atmosphere of a properly constructed magic circle would be unpleasant to them. If malicious, they would not like communion, harmony and respect for life, and in any case, could not get past the Guardian Spirits. There can be no serious breakthrough of negativity while they, not to mention the Goddess and the God, are watching over you.

Our ancestors may have been superstitious about these things at times. But they had another reason for feeling tension at Samhain. If the harvest had been bad, the turn of the year heralded a long period of hardship. Food would be scarce until the following summer. Even if the harvest had been good, decisions had still to be taken about distribution, storage and also the rate at which particular foods should be consumed. Trade matters must have been considered too. Which foods could safely be bartered for other things? Which must be kept? By Samhain, the doorway to winter, all this must have been decided. Had the right decisions been taken? Was everything in order? Our ancestors would have looked for answers and reassurance through divination.

Nowadays, we may still look for messages at Samhain with the same personal urgency, though not always with the same economic or physical imperatives. Today, as in the past, the Goddess as Wisewoman and the God as Lord of Shadows are guides through death's realm and the uncertainty of this most mysterious of all the seasons. The God is Lord of Night, the Old Wiseman, teacher and guide on both sides of the Veil. The Goddess brings a Samhain gift of wisdom, and it may be sweet or bitter to receive, according to our circumstances and desires. As a part of all this, we can consider death as an aspect of our lives. Perhaps some old plan or aspiration needs to die now.

The year's fruitfulness is at an end.
Life has ebbed down into the earth.
There is no thrust of life and, in all nature,
darkness gathers.
Now, with plants and animals and all of life,

the wise turn inwards to the sleeping seeds,
for death is a beginning.
I share this time with the dead
and the unborn.

These or similar words can be spoken at the commencement of your Samhain rite (after you have cast the circle and invoked the Goddess and the God).

Light a candle in the centre of your circle, with the words, *May this light shine in the Inner Realms, as it does in the world. It is the Samhain fire. Those who come to sit beside its flame are welcome.*

Sit in silence, remembering friends or any family members who are beloved to you and who have died. See if you can feel their presence now, or that of any other spirits who are linked to you. (Remember that you may not know all the people who have ever been close to you. Some may never have been incarnate during your present lifetime.) Do not try to force anything. Simply wait quietly and remember. If you do feel any presence or hear a voice, talk inwardly with them as though they were physically present. Express your love, for they will hear you. Then silently give thanks for any messages or advice.

Say aloud:

The Wheel of Life must always turn
and death is preparation for rebirth,
as darkness deeply holds the seeds of light.
We shall meet and know, and remember, and love again.

(The last line is a paraphrase of words spoken in the traditional witchcraft legend called 'The Descent of the Goddess'.)

Then rise (not too quickly) and when you are ready dance around the candle deosil to this chant, or to something like it.

Darkness of deepest night,
filled with the seeds of light. [repeat]

(Do not wear any swirling cloak or robe on this night, for safety reasons. You are dancing round a naked flame.)

Earth the power of your dance and chant into the hazelnuts which you will have placed at the base of the candle. Do this, as at previous Sabbats, by visualizing the gold cone of energy dropping down into the cauldron and there being absorbed by the hazelnuts as gold light. Your wand can be used to direct this cone, pointing it down and passing it a few times over the hazelnuts. Before you crack the first one, say, *Within the silence and the darkness, may wisdom's fruit bring inner knowing. May it strengthen me, as I descend through the darkness of a winter season. I accept the change that wisdom brings, for such fruit may not be eaten lightly. It is the Lady's gift.* Eat the hazelnuts.

If you have some, burn vision incense, which contains herbs that encourage a light trance state. If not, replenish whatever incense you are burning, or light more joss-sticks. Walk deosil to the west quarter, where you will have placed your cauldron, full of water. Sit beside it comfortably and gaze into the water until you see visions or until, with your eyes closed, you fall into a light trance.

If nothing happens, remember that the act of eating 'wisdom's fruit' and gazing deep into the cauldron is an invocation that you should receive some guidance through the winter season, somehow. If it does not come now you may receive it later, as a dream or realization. But if you are relaxed, then almost certainly some pictures will begin to form.

When the trance is ended and you feel ready, rise and go to the altar, on which you will have previously placed an apple. Hold the apple in your cupped hands, saying, *I hold the fruit of the Underworld, which is given to all who know death in any shape, that they may find the seeds of new life. Every end is a beginning.*

Cut the apple in half with your athame, exposing all the seeds, and count them. It is said, traditionally, that the more seeds the better, since each one means new development, and therefore a step forward in your life. Eat the apple slowly,

seeds and all. As you do so, remember this is 'the fruit of death, which brings life'. Meditate upon any aspect of your life which must die, any old ways which you would be better to shed. Consider how the seeds of the next cycle are already present. You are taking them within yourself, that they may grow – the seeds of plans and creativity, to which you will, in time, give birth (and in doing so, will yourself be reborn).

Take up your chalice. Go deosil to the east quarter (which is the quarter of rebirth, for there the Sun rises.) Pour some wine and drink deeply of 'the wine of the cup of life', for yourself and on behalf of all creatures.

Now, for the world, consider what needs to be lost or to die for the benefit of all. Write it in red on white paper, just the name. It might be 'greed', 'pollution', 'militarism', 'famine' or anything else which you have identified as the cause of a problem, however large or small. Burn it in the Samhain fire – the central candle – with the words, 'So may this pass away and leave the world.'

Sit by the cauldron and visualize the birth of new ways, of a just world where food is available for all, perhaps; or a world of environmental harmony; or a world of genuine peace. Whatever you have banished, see it now replaced by new life, a new system, where 'Harm none' is the prevailing code.

And that, apart from a communion, concludes the Samhain rite.

Bright blessings in the darkness,
Rae

New Green
Avonford

27th November 1987

Dear Tessa and Glyn,

You have both, at different times, asked questions about 'rites of passage'. How do witches mark the birth of a child, for instance? Is there a 'Paganing' instead of a christening for witches' children? Do witches have weddings? What about death – when we die, as witches or Pagans, what happens? Is there an equivalent to the Christian burial service? And what do witches believe about heaven, hell or reincarnation?

These questions seem appropriate to the time of year – between Samhain and the rebirth of the Sun at Yule – because they concern birth, sex and death. And then rebirth: regeneration. In answering them, I'll begin with a quote from the witchcraft legend, 'The Descent of the Goddess', because it does show the interconnectedness of these matters; how they are, in fact, a trinity, each implying the other two aspects.

For there be three great mysteries in the life of man, and magic controls them all. To fulfil love, you must return again at the same time and at the same place as the loved ones; and you must meet, and know, and remember, and love them again.

But to be reborn, you must die, and be made ready for a new body. And to die you must be born, and without love you may not be born. And our Goddess ever inclineth to love and mirth, and happiness; and she guardeth and cherisheth her hidden children in life, and in death she teacheth the way to her communion; and even in this world, she teacheth them the mystery of the Magic Circle, which is placed between the worlds of men and of the Gods. [Gardner's Book of Shadows]

By now, it should be obvious that birth, sex and death are

central to witchcraft.

For a female witch, to give birth is to share consciously in the work of the Mother Goddess. For a male witch, to witness and empathize with the processes of pregnancy and birth is to perceive and commune with that aspect of the Goddess who gave birth to all the worlds. During birth, the Veil between the worlds is very thin. It is a magical event. Witch parents will welcome their child, or any child, as an incarnating spirit, acknowledging that this being may be older and wiser than they themselves. If the child is their own, it may not have the spirit of a present or future witch, for the child's religious path may not be that of the parents.

The spiritual reasons for incarnation in a particular family are many and subtle, and often unknowable. There may be a past-life link and people are then able to 'meet, and know, and remember, and love them again'. When this happens it is a deeply fulfilling experience, but it does not imply that all the persons concerned are witches. We have special ties with our own kind, of course, but we would be a sadly isolated group if other witches were the only people we could love.

All these things must be considered before undertaking the task of performing the rite of Blessing for a Witch Child. For the child will not be 'Wiccaned' in the same sense that a Christian child is christened. To try to commit any soul to a path which has not been freely chosen in full adult consciousness would be against all the laws and traditions of witchcraft. So the child may be blessed, and included with the parents on their path, but only until he or she is old enough to make a conscious choice. (In the past, this age of adult discretion would have been considerably younger than it is now. For in the Middle Ages, a boy was thought to be a man from about the age of twelve or thirteen, and girls could be married in their early teens.) The modern Blessing for a Witch Child, or Wiccaning, is meant to last until the child desires to move beyond it, or else further into it, whenever that might be.

When it comes to the planning of the ceremony, first choose the place. A baby may be blessed within a formal magic circle. With a small child, this would never work, because of the problems of keeping small small fingers away from athames and burning candles (and also of persuading a toddler to stay within a nine-foot circle!). Older children, too, may be happier outside. And if we cannot introduce them to the nature deities out of doors, away from any house, then there is something wrong!

Pick a sunny Full Moon day, or Sabbat, and then go into the garden, park or countryside, to somewhere where you think you can be free from interruption. There you can mark out a magic circle with cord or stones. Ask for the blessing and protection of the Guardian Spirits of all the elements, offering a feather at the east, some oil upon the ground at the south, a shell at the west and a stone or some salt at the north. Explain to the child about the life we share with every creature in the world, including those of the plant kingdom; life that has roots in the Earth, as a tree does, and is sustained by Air (wind), Water (rain) and Fire (the Sun), and is upheld by Spirit, the astral shape of the tree, its idea, what you might call the 'dream tree'. This is, of course, for older children.

A meditative child might next be happy to sit with eyes closed while you lead a light trance in which he or she is encouraged to visualize the Mother Goddess and the Father God, and to feel at one with them, watched over and blessed.

Other children might prefer you simply to describe to them the Mother and Father of All, the ones who made the world, and to hear you ask for their presence in the circle.

The blessing itself can be spoken while you place your hands lightly on top of the child's head. Say:

In the names of the Triple Goddess of the Circle of Rebirth, and of the Horned God, I now bless you and consecrate you, Pagan child of the Sun and Moon. I place you in the protection of the Guardian Spirits of witchdom. To them I commend you for safe-keeping, until such time as you are old enough to choose your own path freely. Blessed be!

Here, you should anoint the child with oil on the forehead.

Continue: *I name you* —— [Give the magical name, which the child should have helped to choose, if old enough.] Greet the child with a kiss. Then add whatever prayer seems suitable. For example:

May the light of the Sun and the light of the Moon and stars shine on your path, that you may perceive the beauty of both the day and night. You are a child of the Mother and Father of All, beyond your human parents. Know that every end is a beginning and that the circle of creation has fulfilled itself in you. Know also that you stand within the sacred space between the worlds. Yet that same space lies always deep within you. Wherever you go now, may you find it, as you walk your path in love and wisdom. Pagan child you are, today, but that is not binding upon you. Be as your own being shall decree in future years, in joy and freedom.

You could then share bread and wine or fruit juice, in communion.

Later in life, the child may want to commit him or herself to nature magic, as a witch or some other kind of Pagan. He or she may turn to some other religion altogether, or to none. It is in the hands of the Goddess, for we all have lessons to learn one way or another, and the path of the witch is but one role, one way.

Concerning sex, or marriage, the Craft has this to say. In every happy union, the man finds the living incarnation of the Goddess in his partner, while the woman finds that the Horned God comes to her through the man. And they both enact the loving union of God and Goddess through their desire and its fulfilment. Sex is sacred. Marriage is entered into for love, when there is deep fulfilment mentally, spiritually and emotionally, as well as physically. But the physical aspect is celebrated, as a symbol of complete reconciliation and also because of the heightened consciousness that is attained in ecstasy.

111

Naturally, in a marriage between two witches, there should be no domination of the woman by the man (or of the man by the woman, come to that). A loving equal partnership is the pattern for handfasted witch couples. Handfasting is the witches' word for marrying.

Coven witches would be handfasted by their High Priestess. But as solitary or hedge witches, a couple will not need anyone but the Guardian Spirits to witness their pledges and vows, no one but the Goddess to handfast them to each other.

If either of you should decide on a handfasting at any time in the future, pledge yourself for this life, or for all your lives, according to whether you sense that you are your partner's true friend and lover for this life, or eternal partner, actual 'soul mate'.

Having cast the circle and invoked the Goddess and the God, you can make such promises as you have decided upon, ... *by Air and Fire and Water and Earth, and in the names of the Triple Goddess of the Circle of Rebirth and of the Horned God, Lord of Day and Night.* You should call upon the Guardian Spirits to witness these vows. Then pass your linked hands through incense smoke and candle flames (swiftly) and through water, and then touch them to the pentacle or stone.

Tradition has something to say about handfasting. The couple should hold hands and then jump, together, over a broomstick which has been laid across the circle. If you should wish to end the rite by making love in the circle, so much the better. A communion should follow this.

A couple may choose to be handfasted outside. Then a full magic circle cannot always be cast, nor can you make love during the rite – or not unless you find somewhere unusually remote! But if you make vows in some special place, the Old Gods will certainly bless your union. You can include such magical customs as the drinking of a consecrated wine from the same chalice. What matters is that the vows should come from the heart and that the hands be linked while the union is seen to be real and binding, at least in this life, witnessed by the elemental spirits. (Their presence should have been requested, and invocations made to the Goddess and God.)

Death is the third aspect of this trinity, for death leads on to rebirth. When our bodies are too old or ill to bring happiness, death gives rest and refreshment to the spirit. Death is an aspect of life, like birth and love.

A funeral almost always belongs to the Christian Church, if only in the sense that the body is usually laid in ground consecrated by Christian priests. The other mourners, in Britain, are more likely to be Christian than to be anything else, if anything, and therefore to be comforted by Christian rites. But we can hold our own farewell rituals at some date before or after the burial. This could be as simple as dropping a flower into a stream or river, with an invocation that as it is swept downstream towards the sea, the dead person may find peace.

The Summerlands is where witches believe that they go after death. It is a place of great happiness and beauty, like the Celtic paradise of 'Tír na nÓg'. Entry to the Summerlands may be preceded by stages of purification and learning. After leaving the Summerlands, we may also undergo preparation of some kind, before rebirth.

There are often times of great suffering on this Earth, when we feel that we are in hell and will never get out of it. This is quite enough. Neither I, nor any other witch I have ever met could possibly believe in the concept of eternal damnation. There is no everlasting torment awaiting those who are cruel or malicious, those who do not remember the rule of 'Harm none'. Instead, there is a threefold return of the suffering meted out, in this life or another. The purpose of this is not punishment, but enlightenment, if it can be said to have a purpose. It is actually an effect. To use a Christian phrase, you will reap as you sow. This is simply an inevitable law of life.

To return to possible rites for the dead. You will be able to ask for guidance on the nature of these rites, for each individual person. But a consecrated cord, symbolizing the astral cord that links the soul to the body, may need to be cut for anyone who seems unable to move on from this realm to what lies beyond. Those who remain in what psychics call 'the Grey Mists'.

Where there are no such problems, the lighting of a candle to the brightness of their spirit in all future lives, with a prayer for their guidance and protection and for blessings upon them, may be enough. To me, it would seem presumptuous to do much more than that for a non-witch friend. For another witch, you will want to mark their passage to the Summerlands with a full formal rite: commending them to the care of the Horned God, who is guide in the realm of death, and to the love of the gentle Goddess, who in time gives us rebirth, must form the substance of the rite.

Remember, 'You must meet, and know, and remember, and love them again.' And yet grief is natural and a period of mourning necessary. For never in this world will that same person be seen again with the same face and hair and way of walking, same gestures and same voice.

One day, perhaps, we will all commune with the dead more easily. Our realm will be that much clearer and closer to the Summerlands itself. Meanwhile, I think of it as though they have gone on a long journey. They will be different when in another life, I next see them, and so shall I. Meanwhile, they are like travellers who are sometimes beyond the reach of post or telephone. But usually I can send my love towards them, with the psychic assurance that they still receive it.

Nature dies in the autumn, but she is reborn in spring. The Sun dies each Winter, as the days grow shorter and the light withdraws. At Yule, he is reborn. In life, projects end and ideas collapse, and then something is reborn from among the ruins. This is the universal pattern.

Birth and love and death. As the legend says, these are the three great mysteries, and magic controls them all.

Tessa, now that you have done the self-initiation rite, I greet you as my sister witch. Wise and blessed be. Glyn, I think your decision to wait is a wise one, in view of your plans to marry Laurel. At present, you say, her interest in witchcraft is academic, rather than heartfelt. In future, she may be sympathetic to your practice of the Craft or she may, herself, become more interested. If neither of these two things should happen, then you may have to choose between being a witch and being Laurel's husband. Great resentment can build up when one partner is hostile to the other's religious practice.

I shall risk a prophecy. I do not think that Laurel will remain indifferent, or become hostile. I think, rather, that she will become a witch. At present, I should say that her attitude is not merely over-rational, but healthily sceptical. Having met her, I believe she is a very honest person.

I will keep on sending the letters to both of you, as requested.

Blessed be,
Rae

New Green
Avonford

16th December 1987

Dear Tessa and Glyn,

It is almost time for the Festival of Yule, the winter solstice – magical remaking, recreating time, the birth of life and light. Between Samhain and Yule, the Lord of Night has ruled and been our guide through the realm of shadows. And the Goddess, as the Crone, the Old Wisewoman, offered us wisdom and dreams. In the unblossoming, ethereal landscapes, she has shown the enchantment of this season. The year died at Samhain and the time since has been spent withdrawn in the mist and shadows of winter. We now prepare ourselves and our home for the Festival of Yule, for rebirth.

The metaphor is clear. While we are withdrawn, in death or in the inturned burrowing of the winter season, inner realms expand. The richness of imagination, astral worlds and dream states, where the seeds of the next phase are to be found, are lit for us; they bring illumination and restoration. All this is symbolized by the glamour of Yuletide traditions and decorations, which predate Christmas, but have been preserved as what are now thought of as Christmas customs. The candles, holly, mistletoe, Yule logs and feasting all come from a much older tradition than that of the celebration of Jesus' birth, and show both the richness of inner worlds and also the passage back into life; active, manifest life.

This day is the Sun's 'birthday'. The longest night of all the year will pass and at dawn, when the Sun next rises, the year will have turned once again towards longer days. It is this we celebrate, the passage back into light from the darkest point, for this means continuing life, a new cycle.

Yule is about the rebirth of the Sun and all of nature, therefore of the new year. There is much plantlore associated with it. Holly represents the old Lord of the Waning Year, the Dark King who, at Yule, is transformed into the Infant

116

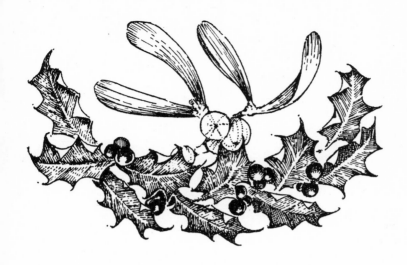

Light. The Yule log, being of oak, is sacred to the newborn Lord of the Waxing Year, as is the robin redbreast. Mistletoe, which is sacred to the Sun, is used as Yuletide decoration by Pagan and Christian alike. It invokes fertility, and the healing powers of summer sunshine.

A witch would therefore decorate the home with holly, mistletoe and other decorations and have a 'Christmas tree' like anyone else, but with a different understanding of why we do these things. (The Christmas tree, as we know it, is a relatively modern tradition in Britain, dating from the last century. But sacred trees hung with offerings are as old as mythology.)

Then there is the tradition of gift-giving. It is represented in the Christian story by the three wise men, gift bringers. In northern folk tradition there is Father Christmas, Saint Nicholas (Old Nik?) with his reindeer, sacred to the Horned God. All children start out in life with a certain inheritance, their range of gifts. Now we are all newborn, in beginning a new year. And this is the real reason why we all give and receive presents at Yuletide. For the same reason, we cover the tree in lights and decorations, heaping the presents round it, acknowledging the gifts the Mother and Father of All Life will bring to us. And we honour the Goddess by placing, right up at the top of the tree, the traditional fairy (representing the Goddess herself) or else a five-pointed star representing nature magic.

And what of the celebration of the girl child's birth. Why does the Goddess only ever give birth to a baby boy? She doesn't, of course. But in the rebirth of our Craft, true understanding of the year's unfolding is still developing, still being found out anew. One thing that is still unrecovered is the yearly celebration of a daughter's birth, the Goddess bringing forth her own self. For at each year's inception, not only the Sun God but also Mother Nature is reborn. She comes to us later, at Candlemas, as a young girl. She then represents not only the spring flowers of the Earth, but the feminine aspect of the Sun and the Maid aspect of the Triple Goddess of the Moon: the springtime solar and lunar Goddess Bride. Girls have mothers too.

The celebration of her birth has been swept away in the long patriarchal years. Certainly, there are Pagan traditions involving a daughter's birth, not least the Italian witchcraft legend of the conception and birth of Aradia. And there are precedents for celebrating the girl child's birth at Imbolg, as 'baby Bride'. But to me, that confuses the theme of her presence as maid. At Yule, however, her birth is sometimes celebrated as twin to her solar brother. And I have heard the hint of a heretical Christian legend that Bride was born as twin sister to Jesus, at the winter solstice. Bride is, of course, a Pagan Goddess predating Jesus by a very long time. Nevertheless, the legend *appeals* to me, for it strikes some chord. Can we now celebrate the daughter's birth at Yule, without obscuring the clarity of the Rite of the Returning Sun? Yes, I think we can.

After invoking the Goddess and God, a solitary witch might go deosil to the west quarter, and then anoint him or herself with water on the forehead, where the 'third eye' is said to be, the mystic centre of all psychic perception, inner seeing. You should then go to the cauldron at the centre, and sit down. Remain quiet for a while, and sense the darkness and silence all around you, the cold night outside.

Say, *On the longest night, all nature sleeps. Coldness and stillness like death grip the Earth. There is a reign of darkness. There is a pause, a hovering between life and death, a suspension. But the world is ever dreamt awake, year by year. Silver vision be granted to me, in this darkness. I share in the work of Mother Goddess and dream the future into being.* (Glyn, you should change the last line of this invocation, saying, *Silver vision be granted to me now, in this darkness, that seeing the dreams of the Mother Goddess for life on Earth, I may celebrate and dance them into being.*)

Close your eyes and go into trance, repeating to yourself,

> *For as the world is dreamt awake,*
> *from year to year and age to age,*
> *and the Sun shall come up early,*
> *may silver vision be granted to me,*
> *in this darkness.*

Repeat this until the pictures begin to form. See the world as it could be if peace and harmony were restored everywhere; if the Goddess were honoured and if the Horned God once again sang aloud in joy and freedom, while all life danced. See how the world could be, as the Sun rises, a faint gleam at first. Then imagine rays of sunlight over the land, revealing Earth in unspoilt beauty. What is this world like? How do the people live? What is their relationship with the other life forms? What is valued now? See the art and hear poems and music. See the expression of love. Then see if you have a part to play in creating this world. Dream yourself acting or invoking for change. See the results.

Now rise and stand with your back to the altar, saying,

> *I dance for birth, for the returning Sun*
> *and for the Earth in dawn beauty.*
> *Now the womb of night gives birth to life and light*

and all shall be renewed. It begins here, now.
Womb of the night brings forth new life and light.

Repeat the last line, as you dance deosil, building power and energy. Direct this into your cauldron. Inside, there should be an unlit candle and some clippings of fir. The fir twigs are then taken out and arranged around the cauldron in a circle. Say these words:

> *The circle of life is unbroken in the Triple Goddess. In her, life is renewed and so light shall return. For the Great Mother gives birth to the Son and Daughter, now, in a timeless moment. Sun child and daughter of the Earth are seen, as worlds are recreated. Hail to the Sabbat of Yule!*

Light the candle, saying, *May the morning be greeted with joy. For behold! The newborn Sun shall arise.*

Take your wand and pass it through the candle flame. Go deosil around the circle, waving it at each quarter, with the invocation, *Peace on Earth. Life and light to all.*

Return your wand to the altar. Then go to the east, with a bell. Say, *The cry of the newborn Daughter of the Earth is heard in all the worlds. Now celebration bring renewal, a new order, in her name. Blessed be!*

Ring the bell at each quarter. Hear it echoing on the inner planes, as well as travelling to the four quarters of the Earth, on the four winds. Replace the bell upon the altar.

Next fill your chalice with honey water, or with wine flavoured with honey. Hold it up before you, and say:

> *I share in the renewal of all life.*
> *With all creatures, I am cherished*
> *by the Mother Goddess.*
> *May I grow in —— [for example, love and wisdom].*
> *Pagan child of the Sun and Moon.*
> *I am reborn in freedom.*
> *I am nourished in sweetness.*

Drink from the chalice. As you do so, meditate upon the theme of development, the nurturing of gifts, abilities. There will be some Yuletide gift from the Goddess and God to help you on your way. Close your eyes as you sit silently beside the cauldron. See the Mother and the Father of All Life. Picture them coming towards you, in the dark, snowy night. You are in a forest, with stars shining above you between bare branches of trees. You meet the Lord and Lady in a small clearing. Held towards you is the gift, or gifts. You may see something clearly recognizable and know at once what it is. Or the gift could be represented symbolically. Perhaps it is something abstract. If you do not know the meaning, ask for understanding. Receive the gift with thanks. This will come to you later on in the year. Now open your eyes slowly. End with a communion.

That is a winter solstice rite. Be merry and wise and be renewed.

Well, I have now introduced you to the meaning of all eight Sabbats and of the Moon celebrations. In neither case is there any linear progression, but a circle. Our understanding of either sequence can change, collectively or individually. And relationships between the two, between the Sun cycle and the Moon cycle on Earth, are still too little understood and must be felt for, intuited.

There is nothing final in this version which I have given you in my letters. It is simply what Cole and I have been doing this year. Next year, we may have changed, may be celebrating in other ways or with other emphases. In the Mother realm, things shift shape.

One more letter will follow.

Bright blessings,
Rae

1st January 1988

Dear Tessa and Glyn,

In answer to your questions, there is something impenetrable about the winter solstice, a transcendence and mystery. In a timeless moment, all of nature dies and is reborn. It is like the beginning of all time, the first creation of all the worlds, the many levels of reality and existence, both manifest and unmanifest, objective and subjective. I can't tell you how it happens; but the cycle of the year, which we celebrate, is Goddess and God made manifest. At Yule, we must acknowledge their transcendence. The Goddess is unborn, she never dies. Between the worlds, she is eternally creating. Thus, she gives birth to the worlds afresh, at the end of each cycle of time. It is this we celebrate at Yule, as the birth of a New Year. The cauldron is the symbol of the mystery. It is within the cauldron of the Goddess that the Dark Lord is transformed to Infant Light. The cauldron is both tomb and womb and is the vessel of transformation.

At Imbolg, the young Goddess Bride and the young Sun God are Daughter of the Moon and Son of the Sun, here on Earth. And we celebrate the God and Goddess immanent, indwelling the universe. These are not different deities from the transcendent Goddess and God, just as you are not different from your own actions and behaviour. Creation reveals them, just as the endlessness of outer space reveals the infinity of inner realms. There is one Goddess, three in one. There is one God, Lord of Day and Night. We meet them in many guises and we know them by many names. These, and the many names by which others know the Goddess or God, are all sacred.

Tessa, you have asked about herbs, incenses and oils. There are specialized books on the subject but I will tell you a little, as an introduction. For you are right, what use is a witch who knows nothing about the magical properties of herbs?

Much knowledge can be acquired by simply looking around you. Which flowers are blooming at any particular season? What colours are they? Which trees are evergreen? Much can also be seen in folk custom and tradition. For example, red roses are emblematic of love. Garlic is well known in connection with exorcism. (Less well known is the fact that it can be taken on trips over water, as a charm against drowning.)

The blending of incenses is a whole craft in itself. It is possible to create a special one for almost any use or occasion. You might become interested and skilled in this aspect of magic, but Cole and I tend to burn only pine in winter and lavender in summer. For simplicity's sake, we vary this only if a particular rite or spell calls for the use of a specific incense – if, in other words, the burning of an incense is the main physical means by which the spell is cast. For example, when purifying the atmosphere in a room, pine, juniper and cedar would be a good blend. (You might find this useful to remember when moving into a new house.)

For trancework, you could burn bay leaves, or mugwort and wormwood. You might want to wear essential oil of lemongrass, as this opens the psychic centres. Just before scrying or reading tarot cards or before any other form of divination, you could drink rosemary, thyme or yarrow tea, as these encourage clear perceptions and the development of clairvoyance.

These are all gentle, harmless ways of receiving the magical benefits of herbs and oils. The stories that some covens in the past used hallucinatory herbal potions, and that they covered themselves in ointments, the famous 'flying ointments' that induced visions, are all true. Very few modern covens still use hallucinogens, but in any case, it would not be wise to attempt their use on your own, without specialized knowledge. The use of a gentle herbal magic, though slower, is as effective. It means less reliance on the physical effects of herbs and more on the etheric and aesthetic vibrations. The main magical tool is then you yourself – your ability to make contact in the inner realms, and to focus, visualize. This is honed by practice and experience. Herbal magic can be an aid. I believe a more forceful approach manipulates the plant spirits and one's own psyche. It can also be dangerous, wrenching the psychic centres open too suddenly, and therefore damaging them. However, a herbal magic which links plant 'vibrations' to trance and inner concentration is both safe and potent, if less obviously dramatic. Anyway, it is what I recommend to you.

Here is a brief list of herbs, with some of their magical applications.

Healing:	rosemary, eucalyptus, peppermint, thyme, sandalwood
Purifying:	pine, juniper, cedar, lavender, hyssop
Love:	rose, southernwood, myrtle, meadow-sweet, basil
Clairvoyance:	bay, mugwort, wormwood, yarrow, rowan
Psychic protection:	asafoetida (smells awful!), cypress, frankincense, garlic, vervain
Luck:	heather, holly, Irish moss, nutmeg, oak

Essential oils for the same purposes would be these;

Healing:	rosemary, sandalwood
Purifying:	lavender, myrrh
Love:	rose, jasmine
Clairvoyance:	lemongrass, saffron
Psychic protection:	cypress, frankincense
Luck:	apple blossom, lemon balm (melissa)

Herbs, with or without oils, can be burned as incense or sewn into sachets and charm bags. Oils on their own can be used to anoint oneself, someone else, or an object (for example, a candle or wand).

At each festival, certain flowers or fruits are appropriate on the altar, or in the room. They may not always be available, in which case you should look for alternatives.

> Snowdrops for Imbolg
> Daffodils for Eostar
> Hawthorn in blossom at Beltane
> Roses at Litha
> Hedgerow fruits at Lughnasadh
> Corn at Mabon
> Apples and nuts at Samhain
> Holly, oak and mistletoe at Yule

These are some of the flowers and trees sacred to the Moon: gardenia, jasmine, lemon balm, wild rose, lily, loosestrife and willow. For a rite of the Moon, any of these may be suitable.

It is now up to you Tessa (and to you Glyn, if you do take self-initiation in the future) to rediscover and to recreate the old Craft of the wise, as solitary or hedge witches. This means walking a path that the world, in general, will still barely acknowledge. It is a path of wildflowers, candlelight and starlight. It is also a path of bloodroses, stoneroots. Much may be asked of you, but you will know the mysteries. The cup of the wine of life will be yours to drink and the bread of communion will be yours to eat, even if, at times, there seems to be not much else on the table. Your life will become a quest in which every kind of experience has meaning.

> May the blessings of the Triple Goddess
> and the Horned God be upon every step that you take.
> Rae

Part Two

Ladywell
Hillsbury

19th March 1988

Dear Tessa,

Happy Eostar! It would be wonderful to see you for the weekend. Come in the summer, when the weather will be warmer and we will be more settled in. I think that you will like the house. And the town is very different from Avonford: much quieter, and the country seems to come in right through the door.

I don't think I can give you the new lessons on the subjects that you've asked for in such a short time as one weekend. When it comes to your further learning, I think we should resume our old way of lessons in letter form. It does help me to have a record, as I have said before. And you will be able to take your time.

You have asked about the inner work of the witch. That mysterious word 'trance' which I use now and then, what does it really mean? It has a direct connection with the power to cast spells. And it also means a state in which the future can be divined, and the spirits of nature communed with. By it, changes are wrought. But is it used outside of the circle, in ways which I haven't yet told you about? Yes it is. Trance is the inner magic, felt communion with the sources of all our lives. It is also a means of transformation. For what is changed in trance, imaged or 'seen' differently, is always followed by outer change, if the image is accompanied by sufficient emotional 'charge'. Do not forget this, for you can tamper with your own mood, for good or ill, in trance, and even with your own health, as has been discovered by alternative health therapists and psychotherapists worldwide.

To a witch, trance is the real essence and soul of all magic. And it is often undertaken where ritual is not yet appropriate – when the witch is unprepared for ritual and needs to meditate or to seek more guidance or to become sure of his or her purpose. And if the performing of rites is the outer work,

129

then trance is the inner work that any witch must do. In trance, he or she can can always find the Goddess and God, and find the Way, anywhere, and not just at set times and within the magic circle. Trance is the witch's real source of ability.

Before you had experienced the festivals of the turning year and celebrated phases of the Moon, you had no signposts for journeying in Inner Realms, no outer map from which to trace an inner one. And until you had perceived the Goddess as creator and sustainer of all life, with the God, her consort, as both co-creator and guide, you had no spiritual points of reference. I don't mean at all to imply by this that those who are not witches have no spiritual reference points. There are other Ways. There are many other Ways. But to venture upon inner paths without *any* frame of reference, any true knowledge, is to risk emotional and psychic instability.

You may wonder if I exaggerate the dangers. I do not, for witness the young people who have opened psychic centres by the use of drugs in wrong circumstances and with no inner orientation or knowledge. Personalities have been shattered and damaged lives have been the result, for astral disintegration, a falling to pieces psychically, does manifest itself, is lived out in the 'real' world, and in great pain and confusion. A witch need not run that kind of risk, for he or she encounters astral beings and events with knowledge and respect, and with psychic skills. That sense of the sacred, which is the first condition of respect, is innately yours. No one could truly be a witch without it. But the knowledge, as you have rightly said, is still something you don't have. Nor do you have the psychic skills. I can teach these to you, and then you will be safe.

When you are experienced, you will no doubt take astral risks of your own choosing. They will be taken advisedly, on the strength of sound judgement. Meanwhile, I can be to you the teacher of basic techniques (be an inward-bound instructor?).

The first trance exercise may seem undramatic, after these warnings, but it is worth working at. I want you to lay down pathways and create a safe place to return to or go from, a clear sense of orientation.

You have already done some trancework at the Full Moons and festivals, and what I shall teach you at first is really very little different, though it will become more complex. The aim is to get beyond pre-planned routes, where everything is decided before you go into trance. Eventually, you will be able to travel and explore simultaneously, for the purpose of resolving conflicts in yourself, receiving guidance, metaphysical instruction or a healing, or for working magic of a most subtle kind, the 'dream spell' kind of magic.

Just about every religion in the world makes use of trance and meditative techniques in one form or another. These soothe the logical mind, lulling it into quiescence, so that the transrational can appear and reintegrate. Mantras, mandalas, repetitive prayers and the rosary, drumbeating, drugs and special yoga positions are some of the many techniques used to gain altered states of consciousness. As solitary witches, we do it ritually by creating a sacred space and by dancing and chanting within it. But we can also move into the same 'lucid dreaming' state by entering trance through a vizualisation, a mental routine that directs us inwards and deepens the consciousness, working as simple self-programming. In other words, the initial visualization instructs the mind, 'Turn inwards.' And so we do. The best way to understand this is to try doing it.

As with any other magical activity, you must be free from interruption. Take the phone off the hook and put a sign on your door, if necessary, requesting all visitors to come back tomorrow. Dress warmly, as your body temperature will fall in trance. Heart and breathing-rate both slow down, as in sleep. Sit somewhere comfortable in a relaxed position. An easy chair with a fairly straight back is ideal for this. Do not cross your arms and legs. And now relax.

You may need to do a simple relaxation exercise, like the clenching and releasing of all muscles. Start with your feet, tightening all muscles up to your ankles. Hold tight and then let go. Move on up through knees and thighs. Clench each in

131

turn, and then relax. Then the muscles in the stomach, buttocks, chest and shoulders. Each time, clench and relax, taking it slowly. Then arms and hands. Then neck and jaw. Finally, clench all the muscles in your face. Then clench everything and relax, all over.

This is a common relaxation exercise. And if you have another favourite technique, then by all means use it. In time, you will not need to use anything, but will be able to go into trance at will.

Now mentally cast a sphere of blue light around yourself, the same kind that you cast around your magic circle. Visualize it. Then say to yourself:

I cast around me now a sphere of blue light, like the cloak around our Mother Earth. May this protect me. I am of the Earth and sky, child of the Great Mother. May she and the Horned God, watch over me. May I be guided in Inner Realms, where endlessness of time and space is mirrored by reaches of furthest stars.

If this is too long, or if for any reason you don't like it, make your own invocation, but along these lines.

You may wonder why you need to take your own atmosphere or protective barrier, just as if you were going deep-sea diving among piranha fish! Well, most of the time these precautions are not necessary. But sometimes, you will be thankful for them. Inner realms, you see, are created by the imagination. Or, to put it more accurately, they are both mirrored and perceived by it. But that does not mean that *only* your imagination and its products are to be encountered. Since imagination is the medium in which we meet any archetypal force, it transcends our own realizations. And the archetypal force may have been shaped into a being called an 'entity'. This is, in fact, a thought form ensouled with archetypal strength and nature. It will have an independent existence beyond *your* imagination, because the collective imagination goes on perpetuating it. You may also meet the imaginative products of the personal desires and fears of people close to you. As if this were not enough, you may meet the repressed aspects of yourself, those areas of being which you may have disowned and cut off, and which are prowling around, angry. Of course, the point of trancework is to reconcile or transform these situations. But it is not done by allowing to untransformed, unwelcome psychic visitors a kind of free posession of your psychic space.

True imagination is the realm of Ether, and what happens there determines physical reality. This, after all, is the basis of all magic. But conversely, the conditions of our lives affect imagination. The archetypes of militarism, for example, are strengthened by glorification of actual war. And images in pornographic videos feed archetypes of violence against women. The creation of an atmosphere of love and wisdom which goes with you and sustains you is therefore as advisable as the wearing of clothes in the street. And the requesting of Guardian Spirits to keep you clear and calm is really common sense. The Inner Realms are not all sweetness and light, for if they were, the whole world would be innocent and we could all go home to the Summerlands, our manifest existence over (until the next cycle?).

If your trance is not to be especially deep, but is a matter of a simple request for guidance over some decision that must be made at once, then the blue sphere of light will be enough. But for more serious trances, I shall repeat, you should also invoke the protection of the Guardian Spirits of Air, Fire, Water and Earth, as though you were constructing a full magic circle, but in your imagination. Make a request at each quarter, that they watch over and guide you. You may also visualize placing your offerings at each quarter, as when you are casting a spell outside of the circle. See incense, candle, water and stone. Ask the Guardian Spirits to go with you, until the trance is ended.

The blue sphere will remain around you after you have ceased to visualize it. You are not meant to see everything through a blue haze. Simply state that it is there. In the realm of Ether, existence follows thought immediately. Because you have given thought, it will remain there, just as long as you have said it should.

133

That done, visualize that the floor you are standing on is no longer of carpet or wood, or of bare boards or stone. You are standing on green grass. There are no walls around you; instead there are tall trees. And you are now within a clearing in a wood. There are leaves on all the trees and the birds sing. Here, you can meet with your familiar spirit, prepare for further journeying or be at peace. There are wildflowers among the grass. Walk around and look and smell the breeze and hear the birds sing. Hear the sound of wind in trees. Overhead, there is blue sky. Take off your shoes. The grass beneath your feet is fresh and the Earth upholds you. Feel the Earth's energy pouring up through the soles of your feet, filling your body. You feel strong, you are yourself, witch and priestess, dressed in your robes. Your hair is loose and your athame is in your belt.

There is a wooden altar at the north side of the clearing. On it, there is wine in a chalice and bread on a wooden plate. Point your athame at the wine and then state in the names of the

Triple Goddess and the Horned God that it must reveal its true nature, and demand that that nature be shown. If the wine then glows with a brilliant light of gold, silver, white or rainbow colours, you may pick up the chalice and drink the wine. But if it is murky and stagnant-looking, ask the Guardian Spirits of Fire to assist you. They will at once create a fire in the clearing, like a camp-fire, small and contained, but glowing. Fire is the element of swift transformation and purification. What you are doing here is to change your religious emotions from unfulfilled and unhappy feelings to joyful ones. By religious emotions, I mean primarily that sense of communion with all the natural world which is the main Pagan spiritual impulse. The chalice contains communion wine and the bread is, of course, communion bread.

Repeat the same procedure of 'checking out' the true nature of this bread and also place this into the fire if it looks dull or mouldering. But if it shines with a brilliant light, then eat it.

What to do if bread, wine or both have gone into the fire? Wait a while and they will reappear on the altar. Check each one again. It is most likely that they will be all right this time. If they are not, then you will have the basis for a meditation on whether you are suddenly uncomfortable with Pagan worship, and if so, why? You may need to come out of trance while you think about this or stay in your inner place while you ponder. (If you do come out, then you must follow the usual routine for opening the circle and for sealing your own aura. But I shall describe this, shortly.)

More probably, the bread and wine will be shining. As you drink and eat, feel the life of the woodland around you. Birds in trees, and moles and mice and all small creatures in burrows. Butterflies and spiders and flies. Worms and the unseen bugs and beetles, and beneath the earth, rocks, underground streams. All around you, the flowers and trees and the nature spirits, those who tend the woodland and watch over you – for you are also of the Earth, child of Mother Earth.

When you are ready, say a silent prayer of thanks to the

Goddess and God. Leave the chalice and plate on your altar. (Whenever you come back to them, they will always have been refilled.) Take a farewell look around at the woods and then feel the earth becoming floor again. You are returning to the circle you had cast around you, in your room. Thank the Guardian Spirits of Air, Fire, Water and Earth. Bid them *Hale and farewell.*

Draw the blue circle in around your body, so that it follows the contours of your own shape, like a second skin about three inches deep. Visualize a skin of gold light over that. State:

> *This aura of blue light that is edged with gold shall remain with me now, as I go forth into the world. In the names of the Triple Goddess of the Circle of Rebirth, and of the Horned God, may I be protected, as the tree is by her bark, the fox is by her fur, and as the Earth is by her blue atmosphere. So may it be.*

Add anything else that you may wish to say, or else make your own prayer. Slowly open your eyes, and get up, slowly.

That is enough for a first trance outside the circle. As you can see, it is far simpler than the one you undertook at your initiation. The entry is more complicated, because you do not have the physical routine of casting a circle, nor the process of invoking the Goddess and God, to turn your consciousness to Inner Realms and to attune you to the presences of the deities in everything. On your return, you do not have a magic circle to come back to, either, just a room in the everyday world. You must therefore ease your way in and out much more carefully.

I must stop now, or this letter will become a thesis! Write and tell me how you got on, and when I may expect your visit.

Blessed be,
Rae

Dear Tessa,

I have more to write today, so I have decided to send this in the same envelope as yesterday's letter. It does seem a good idea to send a lot of information all at once. You will not want to make one small experiment in trance, and then reply to me by post and perhaps wait weeks before you can try out the next stage. I will send you the lessons in batches. You can reply by phone instead of letter, and that will speed things up a lot. I know I told you not to rush this all in one weekend, but on the other hand, I do not want you to feel held up.

I will have to anticipate your questions, as you have not yet seen the letter that I wrote yesterday. So I'll imagine you are saying, 'But I thought trance was more than just picturing and visualizing.' So it is. But these preliminary ventures in the creative use of imagination are important. They are practices you will always need.

After a while, things will start happening in trance 'on their own'. Perhaps a unicorn walks out of the woods, without you having consciously decided to imagine it. This is like having a dream, although you are always awake. But it is not like an ordinary daydream. The colours you see will be more intense and the images of an extra-clear delineation. In fact, it is like those visions seen on the edge of sleep, and must come from the same source. But where as edge-of-sleep visions happen spontaneously, trance is a deliberately invoked process. The picturing of things is always an aspect of trance, and always will be. It is the means of invocation, the way you begin a trance, and it is also your contribution while it goes on, your psychic creativity.

It is important to realize that you are never 'taken over', and so conscious choice about what you see or do always remains real. A witch never loses consciousness in trance (unless she or he accidentally falls asleep!). You will not lose contact with your physical surroundings. You will certainly not become 'possessed' merely because you are in a trance state. You will not behave like one of those mediums portrayed on television, who re-emerge into consciousness unaware of what they have said or seen, only to be told by an astonished audience that such and such a dead person spoke through them. No such thing will happen to you. For a witch, trancework means something quite other than that. Any dead people whom you may happen to meet will be speaking for themselves, inside you, as in dreams. But because you are fully conscious, you will be able to relay the information to any third person who may be watching over you in trance, in the same room.

If alone, be assured that if a child wakes up upstairs, you will hear them at once.

As I have suggested, trance, edge-of-sleep visions and dreams are all much alike, and they must come from the same source. But dreams, at least for most people in modern Western culture, are entirely passive. The dreamer has no conscious choice about the events or outcome. And even actions taken by the dreamer have an involuntary feeling. In trance, the dreamer is awake. Therefore conflicts are resolved, by an active participation; choices are made and actions taken consciously; and sometimes this is done by 'imaging' for a known purpose.

Trancework unites the passivity or receptivity of dreaming with the potential activity and self-assertion of waking consciousness – and reconciles them. Too much of the old knowledge about it is still unrecovered. But it is certainly the solitary witch's main source of power in terms of magic. (By power, I mean the power to do, not power over; I mean ability, not domination.) Trance is also the solitary witch's means of self-integration, regeneration, psychic rebalancing and spiritual exploration. It is her communion with the Goddess and God, her spiritual pathway and door to transcendence.

Trance also has much in common with dreams in that my trance, my inner world, will not be yours. While I can give you knowledge of techniques and show you how to start, your experience of Inner Realms will be unique. You may go to the psychic equivalent of China, while I may go to Iceland, or stay here in Britain. Furthermore, the inner world is much the same as the outer one, in that while we are all in the same Universe, we each feel and experience it for ourselves. This means that once I have taught the basic techniques of trance, you may take inner journeys to places I have not seen, or experience the places that I have seen in ways very different from mine.

If anyone tries to impose their psychic experience, or their rationale about it, upon you, then you should regard them with deep suspicion. There is no such thing as the One True Way. (Please never think that I am teaching it.)

For the next exercise, you should sit or lie comfortably, as before. Lying down is more likely to lead you to fall asleep, if you are already tired. But that doesn't really matter. Regard it as another kind of healing if it does happen. Then thank the Guardian Spirits when you wake up. Ask the blessing and the guidance of the Goddess and the God upon your life, and draw the blue light in around yourself, as at the end of trance. If you fell asleep, then you must have needed sleep, and can try going into trance on another occasion.

After you have visualized your blue sphere and invoked protection, feel the forest floor beneath your feet. As before, walk there on green grass and amongst flowers. Look and see if you are wearing your witch's robe, or whatever clothes you were given at your initiation trance. If not, look around the clearing till you can see them. Take everything else off and put the robes on. This is an affirmation of your role as witch and also helps you further to transform from everyday consciousness and to evoke psychic skills. It is something you should do at the beginning of any trance.

Now walk into the woods that lie to the east of your clearing. They will soon thin out and you will find yourself on the edge of an escarpment, looking east. There is a fresh breeze. Breathe this in and then call on the Guardian Spirits of

Air, asking them to carry all false ideas and unhappy thoughts away, dissipating them harmlessly. Feel the fresh air fill your lungs, till the energy runs through your veins and you are now alert and clear-headed. Look into the great expanse of sky that you can see from the escarpment. You may see the Guardian Spirits of Air. If not, request them to appear for you. Then you will see one or more of the Guardian Spirits of all that is young, fresh, of the morning, of waxing Moons and springtime and all beginnings. Ask if there is anything that you need to understand about them. The answer may be something that you can see, for you may be shown a symbol. Otherwise, you may hear a voice or else sense the answer. If you do not understand, ask further questions. Finally, give thanks for this and also for the purification of Air, which you have just been given, and go back to the clearing.

Now go into the woods to the south. You will find a place where Sun strikes through the trees, in a shaft of golden light. Ask that all unease, disease and harmful energy be transformed. As you stand there, feel it burned out of you, as in a fever, but more gently. You are glowing with the energy of Fire, received from the greatest source of Fire we can conceive of. Within the shaft of light, you may see the Guardian Spirits, or one of them. They are of passion and vitality and the prime of life, midday, Full Moon and the element of Fire. Everything bright, glowing and energetic is theirs. Ask if there is anything you need to understand about them.

You may be puzzled as to how the Sun can be the God, and also be an expression of Fire and its Guardian Spirits. The answer is, of course, that the Sun is not literally the God, but is one way the God manifests himself, by means of Fire. The God, the Father of All Life, is the Sun King, the Green Man, the Horned God, and there is something of him in all animal life, and in every man. As Father Nature, he may easily be understood as the Sun, just as the Goddess may be perceived as the Moon or as oceans.

Then leave by a path which goes west. The earth slopes gently downhill now. You will see a spring which feeds a

140

small pool. From this a stream runs downhill and the water is clear, silvery and sparkling. Bend down and drink some, calling on the Guardian Spirits of Water to cleanse and refresh you. Ask them to wash away all false images, all fears and bad dreams. Ask them also to revive you, as witch and priestess. Sprinkle yourself with water, especially on the crown of your head.

Look into the water and around the pool. You may see the Guardian Spirits of Water, or one of them. They may be in the pool, or sitting by it. They are of poetry, magic and dreams. They are of evening, waning Moons, maturity and autumn, but will not look old, for they are ageless. And they are of the seas, lakes and pools and springs and wells. Ask if there is anything you need to understand about them. When you have received the answer, give thanks for it and also for the purification of Water. Go back to the clearing.

Last of all, go into the woods to the north, round behind where your altar is standing. Here you will find a flat-topped rock, which is set firmly in the earth. Sit down on this rock and ask for a cleansing. Call on the Guardian Spirits of Earth. Feel all tiredness, disease and harm drain from you, as the stone takes it. Ask that it be transformed into that which shall feed life. Picture all that drains from you sinking through the stone, down through its root and into earth, deep into earth. Here it will be transformed just as leaves are, or as compost is formed in your garden. Close by, you may see the Guardian Spirits of Earth, or one of them. They are of power and endurance, the Dark Moon, midnight, winter and age, of mountains and all physical creation. Paradoxically, they are of fertile fields and of orchards rich with fruit: all the processes of birth and death and of earthly life. Ask them if there is anything you need to know about them. When you have understood, give thanks for this and for the purification of Earth, which you have just received. And go back to the clearing.

Ether, the fifth element, is centre and circumference, everywhere and nowhere. As you stand within your clearing, you are already within the realm of Ether, being in trance.

141

Find the approximate middle of your clearing, and ask the Guardian Spirits for purification and reintegration. When it comes to the purification of Ether, I usually see a vision of the starry sky and its endlessness. I sense infinity. You may have some other experience. When it is done, ask the Spirits of Ether if you may understand them. It is they who make your vision of the other spirits possible, and yet they are themselves quite nebulous. Give thanks for the understanding and purification.

And now for reintegration and centring. Here, I generally affirm myself as witch and priestess. I ensure that I am carrying my usual staff, am wearing my robe, and so on. I acknowledge myself as child of Goddess and God, upheld by all the elements. Earth energy is rising up through my feet, coursing through my whole body, and then overflowing and fountaining so that it returns to earth – thus making one continuous earth current, one circuit. Air flows in and out of my lungs from all around the wood. Fire and Water are held in a balance, within my being. And so I am ready. I am renewed and strong to return into the mundane world, or else to continue in trance.

This five-fold purification of the elements, and final centring, is very healing to the psyche. It can also improve your health, if done often. And it allows you to deepen in trance gradually, and so prepares you for what follows. But it does also stand on its own, and you may now feel that you have had enough. If this is so, then return from trance. Come back in the same way that I described yesterday, seeing yourself within your room again, surrounded by your blue sphere. Thank the Guardian Spirits and the Goddess and God, and then draw the blue light edged with gold in around you. The first trance meeting with your familiar spirit, which I am about to describe to you, can be undertaken when you are next ready.

If you are ready now, and quite prepared to go on, do not return from trance. You have been attuned, by the purification of the five elements, for what comes next. Remain where you are at the centre of your clearing.

You are now about to invoke the presence of a familiar spirit. This does not have to be the traditional black cat, for a familiar spirit is just another name for a spirit guide and companion in animal form. You will have heard that some witches have manifest familiars. Generally, these are dogs or cats with whom they commune and who may alert them, psychically, to unseen presences. Your spirit familiar may be any kind of bird or animal at all. But its role may be much the same as that of the incarnate familiar. It can accompany you in all future trances, show the way to spirit places you may choose to visit, and can guide and give many kinds of assistance.

Ask in the names of the Goddess and God that your own spirit familiar shall come to you. Say something like,

> *Between the worlds, I call upon you,*
> *my spirit familiar. By Air, Fire, Water*
> *and Earth, I now call upon you.*
> *In the names of the Triple Goddess of the*
> *Circle of Rebirth and of the Horned God,*
> *I call upon you.*
> *As witch and priestess, I now call upon you:*
> *be here now, my familiar spirit.*
> *Now assist me in my true need.*
> *I call upon you, that you now come to me,*
> *spirit familiar, my friend and guide.*
> *From the Goddess, come to me here.*
> *As I am witch and priestess, my friendship*
> *I now do offer to you. Be here now.*

(Of course, there is no need to memorize all of this. Simply say something like it, in your words.)

An animal or bird will now appear before you, your own familiar. It is up to you to form a bond with this being. But if your familiar is truly your friend, it will not be offended if you now point your athame and demand to see it in truth. If your creature responds by glowing with gold, silver, white or a rainbow light, then greet it with love. Tell it who you are, giving your magical name. Make it welcome. Ask its name.

If the creature is not your true familiar but a false guide, visualize a cloud of pale golden light, like the late-afternoon Sun. Point your athame at the animal and then demand that it go into this cloud at once. State firmly, in the names of the Triple Goddess and the Horned God, that it shall do so. Ask that once within this cloud it shall be taken to wherever it most needs to go, to receive the healing and transformation that it appears to need.

The gold cloud will gently disappear and you will find that the creature has gone too. The same technique can be used to banish anything that feels wrong at any time. You are likely to need it.

Occasionally, you may encounter some kind of astral entity that will not respond to your demands to go into a cloud of gold light. Call upon the Goddess and God for help, or upon the Guardian Spirits of Fire. The situation will either be swiftly taken from your hands, or else you will be given extra psychic energy and enabled to deal with it. If you ask for help in a psychic emergency, it is always given. I have never known or heard of a situation where it was not given.

Repeat your invocation and checking procedure until you have a true familiar, and have welcomed them. Remember to ask the name, so that in future you can summon your familiar at any time.

Does the familiar have an objective existence of any kind? Or is it a thought-form you yourself have created, your image of what a familiar is like? Or is it your instincts, seen by your imagination, and personified as animal or bird? I think that any answer is possible, some familiars falling into one category, some into another. But though this is of interest, it is not vitally important. What matters is how you and your familiar get on. In witchcraft it is results that matter, and felt experience as result.

To base any religion upon a belief system is to invite rigidity and to risk an entrenched position. This is because all beliefs are based upon logical constructs and they tend to ignore the transrational and transcendental reality.

144

Ask your animal guide to tell you what you most need to know now; to give you the most useful message or piece of knowledge for you, in your life at this moment. As with the Guardian Spirits, you may be answered in symbols. Strange objects may appear within the clearing. These will have some symbolic meaning, and if you cannot understand then you must tell your guide, and ask for more explanation. You may also sense or hear the answer. It may come 'telepathically'.

Now ask your animal guide if there is anything he or she needs from you. When you have received the answer and responded, bid him or her *Hale and farewell.*

Then feel the earth become a floor again, and see your blue sphere around you. Thank the Guardian Spirits and ask the Goddess and God to watch over you. Draw the blue sphere in around your body. Visualize its gold edge.

Slowly, open your eyes and then begin to move. Slowly stand up.

That was a longer trance than the first, and you may need to eat or drink something to make your body feel completely real again, and thus to 'earth' you.

When you are ready, make notes about this trance. Record it in your Book of Shadows. Include your understanding of the Guardian Spirits; also mention anything unexpected that may have happened, your familiar's name and any guidance he or she has given.

One last word about familiars. They can leave you. Then a new one takes their place, if you make your request again. When they go, it may be because you have changed, and are thus no longer able to work well with that guide. Or it may be that the being that you think of as 'your' guide has now been given some other task, unbeknownst to you. In the event, bid them farewell with thanks, and then make new bonds with the new one.

In trancework, you must both transcend logic and remain sceptical. You can reconcile these opposites in playful exploration, remaining serious about your aims and goals –

which are: a spiritual communion with the Goddess and God; self-knowledge and self-integration; and the development of psychic skills, so that you may fulfil your role as witch and priestess.

Blessed be,
Rae

Ladywell
Hillsbury

27th March 1988

Dear Tessa,

I will anticipate another of your questions: 'What do I do if I can't visualize?' Everyone has trouble picturing sometimes. Either you can't see anything, or what you can see just doesn't last long enough. There are two possible reasons for this. You may be either too tense or too tired.

If you are too tense, try taking longer over the relaxation exercise. And afterwards, just sit with your eyes closed and don't try to go into trance for a while. As you sit there quietly, just day-dreaming, you will see pictures with your 'mind's eye'. Let these happen. And take as long as you need with them. When you feel ready, start visualizing your blue sphere of light.

If you are really too tired, it is not wise to go into trance at all. You may fall asleep, and that is fine. But you may also remain awake, unable to deal easily with any psychic interference or 'false guides'; unable, also, to transcend your own psychic confusion. We all have a level of this. It is unavoidable in a fragmented culture which assails us with distorted and inconsistent values. Falling asleep spontaneously, and so avoiding this problem, may be taken as a healing gift from Goddess and God. But if you *know* that you are much too tired, then it is wiser to rest than to try undertaking trance work.

Sometimes, you may go into trance feeling bright, but find that all the images become hazy and that you have become tired. Ask for help about this. Recently, I had that problem in trance, so I asked the Goddess to help me and she gently removed a black blindfold from over my eyes. I hadn't known it was there, but after it was removed I could suddenly see clearly. This trance was about an exploration of the big question, 'Where does evil come from?' I thought that perhaps I had feared the answer and had put the blindfold on

147

my own eyes. It is also possible that I had been conditioned to perceive this question in one particular way. The taking-off of the blindfold may have been the removal of that conditioning. I didn't stop to ask. Other things were being shown to me which were of a great deal more interest.

You will be wondering whether I really believe that the Goddess herself appears in trance, in person. Well, yes I do. For deep within myself, I carry a spark of her, as do we all. Whether the image that I see of her is just my own, or whether what I see is an archetypal image, held and upheld by many, seems to me to be unimportant. I reach her and she reaches me, in either case. That image, even if I have created it, is an expression of something outside as well as inside myself. She transcends my being, even though she is immanent in me. Thus, the question of whether what I see is subjective or objective becomes irrelevant. If I lived on a planet where we all had green skin, I'd see the Mother of All Life with green skin too. I'd be right to do so. For on that planet, that is how she would be. I am of the web of life. I am within the Goddess, and I find her within me.

The Horned God is within me less obviously than if I had been a man, for I can never embody him. But I still have his attributes, just as I have some traits of my physical father. And I am not contained within the Horned God as within the Goddess. Rather, he is the one who travels. He motivates me. For he breaks in upon the Goddess's autonomy, and then they are both changed. Thus, life goes on. She creates life, then the God is reborn, constantly and anew (while her autonomy is always remade).

This process is the alchemy of both sexes, in their own selves, and applies whatever our sexual preferences. Each person, whether man or woman, has inner polarity. And the inner marriage brings completion, integration as a whole being. This does not make irrelevant but complements the search for a true partner, the true soul-mate.

In the next trance, you are to meet the Goddess as you perceive her. Visualize your blue sphere of light and ask protection of the Guardian Spirits. In your clearing, call your familiar. Ask it to show the way, so that you may find the Triple Goddess, meeting her in each of her three aspects.

You will leave the clearing and follow a winding, downhill path, until you see a cave. The entrance is not much more than a crack between two rocks. But you slip inside, following your familiar. A candle will be waiting for you, standing upon a rock. Pick up the candle and look all around. The cave is clean. Perhaps it is a crystal cave. The floor is sand. At the back is another opening. You go through and a passage winds away downhill, deep into earth. Go down all the way. You can see all right, because of the candle. At the end of the passage you see daylight. Leave the candle on a rock ledge and step outside. You have reached a new place. You are in a landscape, deep within. This is a place of great peace and beauty. Look around and you will see the sea. It is not far away, across meadows. Now ask your familiar to take you to the right part of the beach. There, you will find pale sand and high cliffs. A freshwater stream bubbles out of the rocks and goes down to

the sea. This is a sacred place. Look around you and then walk to the water. You can paddle if you want to. Up above, sea-birds are calling. You can smell salt.

Now ask the Goddess as Maid to be there on the beach.

You will see a young girl running. She is both graceful and wild. She may wear white or silver. These are traditional colours for the Maiden Goddess. (If she does not wear them, there are reasons for what she does wear. You can ask her. Nothing is fixed or dogmatic within the Goddess realm; but nothing is ever meaningless.)

She stops running and comes up to meet you. This is the wild Goddess. She is called pure and that is because she is sufficient in herself. She is integrity. She is the highest freedom. Her virginity is renewed constantly. She is the Goddess of wild solitude and open spaces and has affinity with all animals and all young. Poetry and enchantment are hers. So also is survival in lonely places and all women's abilities to hunt, make shelters, ride on horseback, find water, go for adventures, break out.

She will not mind if you point your athame and demand to see her true form, so as to ascertain if this is the real Maiden Goddess, and not some sentimental parody, some stereotype of young girlhood. (In fact, if you don't do this, she will probably think you a fool!) Having assured yourself that she is who she appears to be, you can ask any questions about anything that she brings to mind. Ask, for example, how you can best protect your integrity. And ask what she would like of you, that her purity of intent and her freedom may find expression in your life. Thank her for the time that you have spent with her, and ask if you may now see the Mother.

The Maid will lead you further along the shore, to where the Mother sits on a rock, facing out to sea. Be sure to check that this is really the Goddess. She will be robed simply, and may wear red (or she may not. There are no rules. Perhaps she is wearing blue or green. This depends on the way your spirit is attuned. What colour does she wear for you?)

The Mother is the power to love and to create life, and she is boundless. Deeply sexual, she is all eroticism, and her

150

experience of sexual passion weds physical and spiritual fulfilment in ecstasy. Her nurturing of children is an unsentimental flow of deep caring. There is nothing artificial or contrived in her, and her love has an impersonal and detached aspect. At the same time, it is completely personal. Thus, she is epiphany and can birth the worlds. She created you and still sustains you. Ask her anything you like. And ask, finally, what she wants of you, that her life-bringing power to create in deep fulfilment find expression in you. Then thank her for the time that you have spent with her and ask if you may see the Crone.

The Mother will direct you towards the cliffs. There, on the sand, the Crone has lit a fire from driftwood. She can be seen wandering along the beach in search of fuel. She is also collecting shells, seaweed and stones, for magic. The Crone may wear black (or again, she may not). When she sees you, she will return to the fire. You should greet her at once. (Do not forget to challenge her, as you did with the Maid and Mother. Be sure she is the true Crone, Old Wisewoman.) She may show you what she has gathered. She is wise and has the knowledge of all healing. She has also the power to bring things to an end. She is feared, because we don't always like giving things up. But when the Wisewoman clears things, it is to make way for a new growth. She is excellent at clearing out confusion and so making space for a decision, a clear choice. Wisdom is her name. She is therefore a great teacher. She is also a weaver of spells.

Ask her anything that you would like to know. And then ask what she would like from you, that her wisdom and understanding can be expressed in your life. Thank her, and ask for her blessing. Then leave the beach, together with your familiar.

Go back to the cave where you had left your candle. Pick it up and return uphill through the twisty rock passageway, to the top cave, where you can leave it upon the rock. Return from there back through the woods and step into your clearing. Thank your familiar and return to the blue sphere. Thank all the Guardian Spirits and make your usual invocation for protection and guidance, as you step back into the everyday world of waking consciousness. Draw the blue sphere edged with gold in around yourself.

It is important to come back as slowly from trance as you went in. If you do not follow this procedure, you will leave psychic senses open and will feel ragged and quite uncomfortable. (If ever you are interrupted in trance, it is important to sit down alone again, as soon as possible. Then do the purification of the five elements, so that you may feel rebalanced and centred. Afterwards, pick up where you had left off, and re-emerge from trance slowly. Seal your aura, by drawing in around yourself the blue light edged with gold.

So now you have seen the three aspects of the Goddess. As a woman, you are identified with her. If you had been a man, you could still ask the same questions of her, if you had wanted to, because you could know her as your own feminine side. But you could never fully embody her. And so you would approach her as the Otherness, other side of the polarity. (As I said before, this applies whatever our sexual inclinations.) As a man, your experiences of her would have been quite different from those a woman has. In the same way, and for the same reason, your perception of the Horned God as Otherness will mean that your experiences of him are quite different from those of a man.

In the next letter, I will describe a trance in which you meet the Horned God as both young Hunter and old tribal Wiseman. I expect the word 'hunter' makes you curl up in connection with anything godlike; as well it might, when thought of in terms of modern fox- and stag-hunting. But these things are not what is meant. They are a departure from the Horned God's true expression. Both aspects of the God are more difficult for most women to comprehend than those of the Goddess. He may also, in a patriarchal society, be more difficult for most men. This is because there are so many images of gods and godlike qualities around that are distortions of him. As present-day witches, I think our understanding of the God still lags behind our understanding of the Goddess. She has had to come first, after thousands of years of suppression of all Goddess worship. And yet the very fact that male gods have been and still are worshipped in mainstream societies all over the world, does make the recovery and recreation of our image of the Horned One that much more difficult.

Every time that you meet him in trance, you help to bring him back, the true Father of All Life. And so with the Goddess. Each time that you meet or invoke her, in trance, you are helping to bring back her worship, her Pagan world.

Blessed be,
Rae

Dear Tessa,

Let me continue. There is no doubt that the Horned God seems harder to perceive in trance, because we, as women, trust ourselves less to understand him – and, perhaps, because we trust him less. In our culture, images of maleness are so tied up with violence and authoritarianism that it is hard to trust. There is the Christian god, for example, with his propensity for torturing wrong-doers in the fires of hell for all eternity. Even the Pagan gods, since patriarchal times, have been perpetually involved in slaughter as gods of war, giving *carte blanche* to rapists and pillagers. As a matter of fact, the Pagan goddesses of the same era were sometimes also deities of war. But this fact is less familiar to us and so is less of a factor. We can ignore it more easily and invoke a much older being, the Mother of All Life, or Triple Goddess of the Circle of Rebirth.

Suppose we get behind patriarchy to the dawn-of-time male deity? We can then ask, What of the Horned God in an era when wars didn't exist? But can we trust that God to be here now? He has been absent from the world a long time, banished. Can we now bring him back? Can we invoke his return? Assuming that he is unlike all the patriarchal gods of whom we have ever heard, can we also find him relevant? This is not, after all, a remote Age of Gold, but the twentieth century – all too close, it seems, to the Age of Plutonium or Uranium.

Who is this Horned God anyway? As a witch, my only advice can be that you see for yourself. And that you have the courage of the Goddess's convictions. For he is her partner and is also the Father of All Life. The word 'father' is quite tricky, too. You will need to forget all patriarchal connotations, like 'head of the family'. It means simply 'progenitor', with all that implies. It means passion and the dance of life: desire. It also means male nurturer and educator of the offspring. These things are seen in nature. Male sea-horses *give birth* to the young; male lions tend and rear young lions. Patterns and possibilities of fatherhood are very diverse in the natural world.

Once again, you must visualize your blue sphere, ask protection from the Guardian Spirits and feel grass beneath your feet, as you see trees all around you.

Call your familiar and tell it that you wish to find and to speak with the Horned God. (Do not forget once again to 'check-out' your familiar.) Ask it to accompany and guide you, and then leave the clearing. As in the last trance, make your way into the woods and find the cave. If you lose your bearings or have any problems, ask your familiar to give help. As before, you will slip inside the cave, between two rocks. And the candle is there, waiting for you. Pick it up and go down through the twisting rock passageway at the back, down and down, ever deeper. You emerge in the beautiful and peaceful landscape, once again. Leave the candle behind in the lower cave.

This time, you do not go towards the sea, for your familiar will lead you some way inland. This is a wild country, as well as beautiful. There are chalk uplands and belts of trees. Except for the highest ground, it is thickly wooded. Through tangled forest, you will emerge on a bare hillside. You begin to climb up. Once at the top, you can see for many miles. Chalk, flint and tough grass are all beneath your feet. You can see now that you are standing on a long ridge. This, too, is a sacred place.

Now ask to see the Lord of Day, the young Hunter. He comes striding along the ridge, a tall man dressed in animal skins and rough wool. On his head, he wears the horns of a great stag. He may be smiling at you in amusement, for this God is a great joker. Check that he is the true Lord of Day, the young Horned God. He suddenly sits down, indicating that you should sit too. He is slim and supple, and you sense that he could outrun the wind and has great strength. He asks

155

if you would like to hear him singing. This is a natural question for him to ask. You haven't asked him for help, you are not hungry, you are not frightened? Well then, life is for enjoying. Would you rather have a song or a story? Or perhaps you would prefer to dance? Choose the dance, and then you will dance a wild dance with the Horned God, on the bare hilltop, to the music of his low-pitched humming. It is a dance of weird craziness, sometimes a jig, sometimes improvisation. And it seems now that your blood dances, and the far-off hills and all the trees dance too, while the Horned God spins you faster and begins to laugh. Almost, you can ride the wind. Almost, you have feet on the earth and head up in the remote stars. Life pours through you and you can earth it: you conduct life.

Would a male witch dance with the Horned God like this, or is it just for you, priestess of the Goddess, a woman? I don't know. I must ask Cole. But I don't see why not. However, I think it more likely, at a first meeting, that a man would simply ask the God to awaken in him the power of life-dancing. Just as you have already asked the Goddess to awaken her power in you. Perhaps it is the Maiden Goddess who whirls a male witch away, dancing wildly on the deserted beach, while the waves crash and the wind flies and all the salt spray turns silver.

As the dance ends, you flop down again. You are relaxed now. You can ask the young hunter-dancer, the Horned God, any questions. Ask him why he is a hunter, if you want to. He will probably tell you that he hunts to live and not for entertainment, taking what is needed for bare survival. He will tell you that he is also the quarry, and that his being is bound up with the creatures who are being hunted. He is also the stag at bay, brought down and killed. This is a mystery which tells us much about the God, and also about ourselves, according to how we react to it. And it is beyond logic. The meaning can only be sensed deep within ourselves, and not objectified.

Remember that this God is the Lord of Death, as well as Lord of Life. Death as an aspect of Life. He is as sharp as the

flint underfoot, as well as soft as chalk. Flint arrows and chalk pictures. For the artist drawing chalk pictures on the pavement in a city may also manifest the Horned God. Herne playful and creative, Herne defiant, and Herne surviving.

When you have asked all your questions, also ask how you can express and uphold his life principles of wild joyousness and honesty, being true to the instincts – real instincts, as opposed to our false and conditioned responses, real life-enhancing, life-upholding instincts.

Then thank him and tell him that you wish to see the Old Wiseman, who is his other self. He will direct you back down the hill and into the woods. Here you will see the Old Wiseman stepping out to meet you. Leaves may be in his tangled beard, and you may perceive him as both crazy old eccentric and wise astrologer. The horns are still upon his head and he holds a cloak of coarse wool round his body. This is no court magician, but a shaman. He can leave his body at will, and collect the knowledge hidden in tree roots or else howled to the Moon by dogs or danced by the March hares. He has the power of candle flames within his fingers. They glow gold and red as he blends herbs. His healing skills have the power of all elements, and he is also the guide in realms after death, having been there too. In life, he is skill in the mysteries. After life, he is the ancient guide and he brings understanding.

After you have made sure that this is the genuine Lord of Night, by following the usual procedure for checking out, follow him further into the wood. Here, you will see a rough shelter, built out of wood, mud and mosses. He invites you inside. (What do you see there?) Then he lights a candle. It was not dark before, but now it is brighter within the candle glow, and beyond that mysterious, shadowy. The Old Wiseman is quiet, but his presence is not austere. Then he asks you what creature you would like to learn from. A strange question. If you have no idea, then you had better say, 'Whichever I most need to learn from.'

He touches you upon the forehead. At once, you are becoming fox, badger, cat, hen, owl or she-goat or whatever you have chosen or have needed to become to gain further understanding. Soon the change is complete and you have shifted your shape. He takes you outside and you explore the woods, with him beside you. If you are a bird, you soar up into the sky. You need have no fear, because he protects you. More than once, he may help you shift shape again. You may be a fish and swim in a fast river, or else an eagle or otter or hind or even a butterfly. Somehow, the Old Wiseman is never far away. He may speak to you from inside a tree or be in a gust of wind.

Finally, you return to the hut and he touches your forehead one last time. You have your human form again, that of a woman. The candle has burned down a long way. The Old Wiseman looks at you steadily and waits for your questions. You have now learned, perhaps, the art of flying, or the art of being secret or the art of shedding old growth, from bird, animal or snake. Ask him to explain the further mysteries of birds and beasts. Ask about anything that you want to know.

Finally, ask how you may express these magic skills and this understanding in you day-to-day life.

He may also ask you a question. Your must answer it as truthfully as you are able.

Male witches may have this experience not with the Wiseman, but with the Wisewoman, Old Crone who weaves spells. Here, I think that they would simply ask questions, and then ask the Wiseman to awaken in them that feeling for the mysteries that comprises keen delight in magic and a quest for true wisdom.

Thank the Wiseman and ask him for a blessing. You should then return to the cave where you have left your candle. Ask your familiar to lead the way. Go back through the rock passageway, to the upper cave, where you should once more leave the candle. And then go back to the clearing.

Thank your familiar. Return to the blue sphere and then thank the Guardian Spirits. Draw around yourself the blue sphere edged with gold. When you are ready, stand up.

What, you may be wondering, is likely to happen when a male witch meets with the Mother Goddess? I think that perhaps she may ask him to walk with her into the sea. What happens next, I do not know. But I think it is about trust and the interconnectedness of all life. I think that here there may also be the lesson of the whale and the dolphin, mammals whose intelligence may be as great as ours, and whose wisdom is certainly much greater and that perhaps he may have to swim underneath the water.

You have now met the Goddess and God in trance. Do not mistakenly believe there are three Goddesses and two Gods. For you have been a young girl and are now a mother and will one day be an old woman. That does not mean there are three Tessas. So it is with Goddess and God: one Goddess and one God, but more than one aspect.

It seems to me also that we can only understand Goddess and God in relation to each other. For what would it mean to be female in an entirely female world? The word would lose its meaning. Similarly, in a male world, one is male in relation to what? I do not mean, of course, that the sexes should be strictly defined in terms of role-playing. When the Goddess puts on trousers and unblocks a drain, she is certainly still female.

Let me know how you get on in trance. I will send you these four letters all at once. I look forward to hearing from you. Hope your spring equinox, your Eostar rite, was good.

Blessed be,
Rae

Dear Tessa,

Now I have given you the basic instructions. There are many other ways of going into trance beside the one I have described to you. There are also many styles of approach and many other astral places to go. But they are all undertaken along the same lines. Remember this process and you can be free in all Inner Realms. First, invoke protection and then find yourself in a peaceful place, for example in the woodland clearing. Go through a purification of the five elements, say, if you feel the need for one. Centre yourself and affirm who you are, the nature of your spirit and your connectedness with all life. Then summon your familiar and explain to it why you have come into trance. What you need may be guidance or healing or self-affirmation or to work magic, by banishing or invocation. Talk about it in some detail. If you have a complex problem then describe it fully. Do not try to find solutions. Simply ask your guide to take you to whomsoever can most help. This may be to the Goddess as Maid, Mother or Crone, or to the Lord of Day or Lord of Night; or it may be to a Guardian Spirit or else to some archetypal being with whom you have previously never met. (Always check the genuineness of your familiar, and of any Deity or other being.)

On certain questions, your familiar may give help directly. Sometimes, you may not need to ask the familiar to whom you should turn. Perhaps it is a waning Moon and you are anxious about the development of your knowledge and understanding in realms of magic. You will know therefore that the Crone can be of help.

Having explained your problem, let yourself be guided subsequently in trance. You may be offered a healing or transforming potion. You may be asked to bathe in some pool or river, or to wear or take off certain items of clothing, or jewellery. This will be because of their psychic resonance, their affinity with ways of being. For example, the wearing of a brown robe may commit you to practical earth-oriented activities, or to some work with animals. A crown may mean that you are being offered some kind of success in life. But be sure that you know the price. Whatever you are given, be sure that you know the true meaning.

You may also be shown guiding visions; or asked to make some choice; or directed to change something manifest, something about your life. Any kind of thing may happen.

When your problem is resolved (and if it is not, then you should go on asking questions until it is), give thanks for the help, and then retrace your steps. Go back through all the places that you visited on your way in.

Thank your familiar and the Guardian Spirits. Seal your aura, by drawing around you the blue light edged with gold.

With this process, you can go into trance at any time and for any reason. No question is too trivial to ask. If something is bothering you, then it *is* important. Nor is any question too large and metaphysical. Once you know this then you may, like many beginners before you, become quite addicted to trance. This does not matter, as in time you will just naturally ease up. While it is going on, you must be careful that you don't deplete your own etheric energy. Trance can do this. Restore it with good food, physical exercise and a contact with nature (gardening or country walks or else, in warm weather, just lying on the ground). If you don't do this, then you may start to feel 'unearthed' and floaty. Also, you will be easily tired and may be more vulnerable to infections.

Eventually, you will know just when trance is called for, and when it isn't. Then it will find its right place in your life. There is no need to worry unduly about depletion. Etheric energy is seriously affected only if you undertake prolonged trance day after day for weeks. And only then if you don't attend to the basic requirements of good health. Physical exercise is especially vital, as it counterbalances the physical stillness of trance. You may not feel like it, but if you are run down, exercise.

Go wherever you want to in trance. Be an explorer. These paths that I have brought you along are not meant to entrap you in fixed astral routines. They are meant to provide you with a safe base and known trackways, and to bring to you the skills that will enable you to find your own ways.

You have said that you find it hard to remember the order of events in a long trance. Try memorizing key points before you go in. For the trance about the Goddess, these might be:

> Invoke protection. Go to the woodland clearing.
> Call familiar (as usual).
> Cave, passage, lower cave, sea.
> Maid – purity (integrity and freedom)
> Mother – love
> Crone – wisdom
> Return to woodland clearing. Thank familiar.
> Return to blue sphere. Thank Guardian Spirits.
> Seal aura (as usual).

If you still can't remember at the time, you can do three separate trances, one each to Maid, Mother and Crone. But above all, I would say if you forget what was 'supposed' to come next, don't worry. Ask your familiar what he or she would like you to do next. Then go with that. Too much anxiety about 'getting it right' will prevent an easy flow of trance imagery. Besides, you can't get it wrong. Whatever happens, as in dreams, will be right for you. Just remember to invoke the Guardian Spirits for protection and to challenge or check out any being that you meet, and also any food, drink, clothing or other item that you may be offered. You need remember no more than that. If you can remember a long trance sequence – fine. If not, then that is all right too. Let me know if this helps.

Here are some ideas for trance.

1. Finding life's purpose. (Asking the question, 'What am I here to learn, to do or to become in this incarnation?')

2. Improving health. (Seeking guidance, undergoing transformations, visualizing sound health.)
3. Psychic cleansing and rebalancing. (You may have been close to the aura of some person or place which you could best describe as corrupt.)
4. Invoking for love.
5. Healing others.
6. Discovering your true essence (that Self that transcends circumstance and carries over from life to life).
7. Understanding the larger cycles of all life.
8. Communing with nature, feeling at one with life, with all creation.
9. Psychic healing of the environment.
   (The banishing of problems. Visualizing ecological harmony between humankind and all nature. Visualizing ways and means – soft technology, low consumption, organic agriculture, etc. The placing of all within the hands of Goddess and God. Invocations for their assistance in healing of Earth. Visualizing the many routes to fulfilment for all the different kinds of people in the new ecologically harmonious world. Music and medicine, art and sport, magic and love, craftwork and poetry. Diving and caving and the climbing of mountains. Scientific research for the sake of further understanding, and not for the exploitation of nature. Education for education's sake, and so on. A world where adventure and fulfilment are possible for all, in non-exploitative ways.) This last example is a big one, and best done when you have had some experience.

Here is an example of a simple trance that is a kind of spell. It is a healing trance and may be done at any time, for anyone.

Follow the usual method to induce trance. Cast your blue sphere, invoke protection, find yourself in the woodland clearing and then call your familiar. Explain that —— (your friend, partner, child or whoever it is) has need of a healing. Ask to be taken to the Goddess's spring, her healing waters that flow constantly.

Your familiar will lead you to the cave, and then down the passageway to the inner landscape. There, you will be taken a long way inland, to a spring that is by a small hill. There are trees around the spring and they are in full leaf. The sound of running water soothes and refreshes you. This is a tranquil place. You can hear birdsong and wind in the trees. The spring feeds a small pool and then a clear stream.

These waters are renewed, always. For thousands of years, rain has fallen on this land and then seeped through soil and the layers of rock, collecting underground before returning as this sacred spring. The whole process takes thousands of years, and the cycle never fails, the spring never dries up. It is constantly renewed, as you desire now that your friend's health shall be renewed, by the power of the Goddess and her healing waters.

Ask the Goddess for a message, for some guidance about your friend's health. What does he or she need? You may hear something in the murmuring of water, or else see some guiding vision in the small pool. It may relate to a necessary change in your friend's lifestyle, exercise pattern, diet or medication. And if the illness is a mild one, you may later suggest that your friend follows this prescription. If, however, the illness is serious, and your friend is currently being treated by a therapist or doctor, then the suggestion you bring back from trance should always be referred to him or her, for confirmation. There is no need, after all, to say that it came from a trance. Your friend can, for example, simply ask the doctor, 'What if I drank more liquid? Or took vitamin B12? Or tried comfrey ointment?'

Now ask your familiar to bring a chalice. He or she will then disappear, to return almost instantly with what you have asked for. (Check your familiar and the offered chalice. It is at moments like this that the true contact can be lost.) Fill the chalice with spring water. Then thank the Goddess for any guidance. Take the full chalice back up through the cave, passage and upper cave and into your clearing.

Now, visualize your friend. You will see him or her. They will be standing in your clearing, when you have called upon them to come. Ask if he or she will accept healing. Remember that if you are sufficiently deep in trance, you will be able to perceive, by way of this visualization, the *real* state of your friend's mind, and his or her *real* feelings. Your imagination is the medium by which this and any other information is conveyed from your unconscious mind or deep soul, which knows everything, into your conscious mind.

If there is any fated reason why healing is not possible, then send your friend upon his or her way with love. You cannot help them. Sprinkle the healing waters in your clearing, giving them instead to the Earth. Then talk with your familiar about your feelings. (Sadness? Regret? Frustration?) Ask its advice about how to deal with these feelings. You are not likely to receive a sophisticated answer, but that does not mean that the advice will not be worth taking!

In most cases, your friend will accept healing gladly. Point your athame at the chalice. Ask that your friend be shown the true nature of this water. It will then glow brilliantly with light. Give the chalice to your friend, saying, *These are the sacred healing waters of renewal, not my gift but that of the Goddess, from whom they came. As you drink, may you be restored, and may your health be renewed.*

When your friend has finished drinking, bid him or her farewell. Ask your familiar if anything outstanding then remains to be done. If not, ask it to put back the chalice, and bid farewell, with thanks. Return to your blue sphere, thank the Guardian Spirits, and so return to your usual consciousness. Slowly stand up.

Later on, whenever you see your friend, you may pass on any information about diet, lifestyle or whatever it was that you may have received in trance.

Blessed be,
Rae

Dear Tessa,

My last letter brings me to a point of ethics. How far can you go in trance over matters that concern the lives of others?

This is an area that calls for absolute honesty, and the utmost care. Having said this serious and implication-laden thing, I will add that there is a funny side to trance involving other incarnate beings. For instance, when our dog barks at night because she can hear a cat, Cole often psychically projects himself downstairs and gives her a telling-off. He simply visualizes that he is standing in front of her bed and shouting, 'SHUT UP, HAPPY!', and it works. She shuts up every time. This causes us a great deal of amusement, as we imagine how bewildered she must be at Cole's very rapid appearance. Dogs are very psychic, and she would probably be able to see Cole, and can obviously sense him.

However, the same device could be used, or misused, on people. Messages of love, comfort or support, or requests to be contacted, are all possibilities, and all beneficial. A strong statement of a point of view for the purpose of communication is also all right. So is a frank expression of your feelings under duress, for example 'Leave me alone!' But what about implanting thoughts or issuing commands because you have decided this is for the person's own good? Or because you believe you could benefit by controlling their actions? To put it bluntly, this is comparable to black magic. The implanting of a suggestion in someone else's mind, a suggestion or thought which you intend them to perceive as their own, is the psychic equivalent of subliminal advertising. The visualization of a person taking actions or making changes which are beneficial to you, but which you have never discussed with them in life, nor been given any reason to believe that they want, is the psychic equivalent of coercion.

I must add, on this subject, that I have talked to a variety of people over the years about psychism. And believe me, 'subliminal' and coercive techniques are used quite often, in all kinds of situations. None of the people who told me they used them was, in fact, a witch, or occultist of any kind. That is one reason why I believe psychic skills should be more openly discussed. For, at present, a witch or any other person with real psychic knowledge and experience will know how much harm such a practice can cause (and how it may rebound on him or herself), but an ordinary person will not know this. Also, they will not usually sense when it has been done to them. A witch, on the other hand, will sense this, and will be able to throw it off. I believe that much suffering could be avoided if such things were demystified, identified – if our knowledge could be shared. For nothing more is needed than the awareness that such things can happen, as easily as put-downs and manipulations happen verbally. And exactly the same response is appropriate in both cases, a challenge and a repudiation. I do not think such awareness has to give rise to psychic over-defensiveness or paranoia, any more than these emotions are produced in ordinary social relations through the knowledge that some people can't be trusted. They can't. And that is cold fact. However, you are all right if you keep your wits about you. And the same thing goes for the constant and ongoing psychic inter-relatedness between people.

If there are rules, then one of them might be, Never project a thought to anyone at all without identifying yourself psychically. (You can appear before them in trance, or you can project a message in thought, such as, 'It is Tessa who says this.') Then their own psyche can identify you as the source of psychic input. Another rule of thumb is that you should never say or do anything in trance that you wouldn't be prepared to say or do physically. So why not just pick up the telephone or call round? In most cases, that is what you should do. But there are exceptions and you will certainly find them. For example, the other person may be ill; out of the reach of a telephone; unconvinced by your manifest words; or in special need of support on both the manifest and psychic levels.

Do not forget psychic safety codes if you send messages. Surround yourself with the blue sphere, place yourself under the Guardian Spirits' protection and project yourself towards the other person, or call them towards you. And then say your piece. Return and thank the Guardian Spirits. Then draw in the blue light edged with gold around your body.

As you may have guessed, this technique of psychic suggestion is quite commonly used in seduction, and by people who know nothing (consciously) about magic. If you ever suspect that it is being done to you, and by someone in whom you are not interested, you can tell the person firmly, in trance, that you don't want to know. And if they are still persistent, you can cut all psychic cords between you. Point your athame, and demand that the threads linking you to the other person (which may be of social obligation, intimidation, pity, confusion or something to do with finance, to name but a few) now become visible. Then, using your athame, cut straight through them. This will often end all physical contact, in time, as well as psychic relations. But it is rarely necessary to take such extreme measures.

I am talking here about the deliberate willing of another person's compliance, using psychic manipulation to achieve this end. I am not talking about the spontaneous picturing of the beloved, or even the spontaneous projection of feeling towards them. Such things are a natural part of being in love. But it is one thing psychically to declare love and desire. It is another thing to pressurize or to intrude deliberately upon an existing relationship. I suppose you could say that a great deal of this comes down to whether or not a person has good psychic manners. These are really quite similar to good manners in life. (The more experienced you become as a witch, the more you will become aware of who around you does possess them – and who does not.)

Well, I don't know if anyone's in love with you right now, Tessa; but I know that you are not in love, and would like to be. You have asked for a love trance, in order that you may

169

improve your chances of meeting someone with whom you could be happy. Here is one way of doing it.

After the usual entry into trance, call upon your familiar, and then ask to be taken to see the Crone. You will go down through the cave and the passage, and then walk to the place on the beach where you last met her.

Ask, *What can I do to find my right partner, the one I can truly love and who will love me, to the enhancement of both our lives?*

The Crone may remove from you certain links and cords that have been binding you to an outworn relationship, any ties which are obstructing the possibility of a new love. She may ask you to change things in your life, suggesting that you give up an old pattern.

You think it is strange to ask the Old Wisewoman about love? But who has the most experience? And who most enjoys match-making? Listen carefully to anything else that she has to say, any positive advice about places to go to, or new commitments.

By and by, she will direct you to the Maid, who will no doubt question you about what you want from a relationship. What suits you? What are your real needs? And what can you give? The Crone is a grandmother figure. She has seen it all. But the Maid is like a wise and sympathetic young friend or sister. She will ask some astute questions, for she wants to protect your integrity, to be sure that the relationship will not threaten your basic individual freedom to be yourself. Only if this requirement is met will she give it her blessing.

Then the Mother will ask another kind of question. To what do you pledge the creative force, the life force, of your love? Do you want your union to produce a child, or shared work or a joint commitment to nature magic? A joint spiritual work? You must answer this question honestly, as you did all the others. Then a moment will come when your certainty about what you want peaks, and you will know just what it is that you need and are prepared to give. The Mother will offer you some sign or symbol. Check it out with your athame, making sure that it represents the kind of relationship you have asked for. If you accept it, you are committed. The Goddess will ensure that your path converges with the right partner, that is, the one with whom you can achieve the most happiness possible for both of you, in terms of your destiny. This may not be your true 'soul-partner', for he may not now be incarnate. Perhaps his circumstances, or yours, may mean that in this life you can't ever meet.

You can ask about this. You may not get a clear answer, for it is a very loaded question. But if it is the case, you will then be asked if you will accept a loving union with someone else (for this life). Such partnerships are, in fact, the most usual. Life partnership with one's soul-mate is quite rare. But that does not make all other relationships second-best. They can show things that could not be learned with the true soul-partner. This is a little like travelling, as opposed to staying at home all your life.

Did I say some of this before, in the letter I sent you about witches' weddings? Never mind. I think it does bear repeating.

Sometimes, the trance may indicate that a ritual should follow. This could be informal, for example a pilgrimage, or the wearing of certain colours associated with love. Or it could be a formal, full-scale ritual, in the circle, specially designed and tailor-made for this specific purpose. I will explain how rituals are created for this or any other specific purpose in a future letter.

Good luck with the love trance.

Blessed be,
Rae

7th May 1988

Dear Tessa,

Before we get on to the subject of creating rituals, there is one final trance which I want to describe to you. It is about discovering your true self, the answer to the question, 'Who am I?'

Of course, the self has many aspects: shadow self, higher self, inner child, conscious ego, super-ego, and so on and so forth. These are classifiable according to many different systems from both psychotherapy and occult lore. Each system of classification has validity, but it is not wise to use any of them to define yourself analytically, until you know what kind of whole being all these parts belong to. The result would only be confusion.

Let us imagine that you are a plant. On your search for self-knowledge and thus self-integration, you may easily discover that you have sepals, calyx, petals, roots, sap, leaves, stem, etc. But until you have also found out that you are, say, a lavender bush, or a bulrush, this is of limited use. In the same way, you can learn that you have an id, ego and super-ego, or a shadow self, personality and higher self. You will also know that you are a human, just as the plant knows that it is a plant. But do you know about your self, what kind of human being you actually are, what kind of plant? Only when this question has been answered do other pieces of self-knowledge fall into place.

To the Pagans of the ancient world, the words 'Know thyself' said it all. The self is endless, because it partakes of life and is therefore part of the boundlessness of the Goddess's creation (from which it can hardly be separated, any more than a drop of sea water can be said to have meaning outside the sea). And yet, paradoxically, the individuality of self is essential to the diversity of creation, to manifest life. Individuality exists, and we experience it. Unless we understand our own, we are at a disadvantage in a world where holly trees and hazels are quite separate and distinct from each other, and meant to be.

The trance I am about to describe could be called 'Identifying the Self'. Why do we need to do this? Why don't we already know who we are? The answer is probably that, as very small children, we do know, but lack the concepts and language with which to describe ourselves, or to translate transrational information. By the time that we have developed these skills, as adults, we have long since ceased to trust our intuitions, and have been talked out of any true perceptions for the purpose of being more easily fitted into the mould that our parents, teachers and any other authorities believe to be best for us. In other words, by the time we reach the age of so-called discretion, and are expected to make choices about our lives, most of us haven't the faintest idea who we are. We may have known as small children, and will certainly have known before birth. But when we get to the point where we need to know, we don't. And without that knowledge, 'destiny' can seem like an incomprehensible opponent.

The old Pagans meant 'Know thyself' completely: not just your creative self, but also your 'shadow', the dark and destructive bits. These must be owned and admitted; for example, a potential for violence if pushed too far, or a tendency to call something 'diplomacy' if it is, in fact, a downright lie. With guidance, you will discover your own shadow, whatever that might be, and all its traits. It is an essential aspect of self-knowledge and self-integration, the discovery and owning of the shadow self. A rose, for example, has thorns, and some plants are poisonous. A denial of these facts will not help any rose (or foxglove) towards a beautiful or useful life.

But first discover the true nature of the whole plant.

I want you to begin in the usual way, by invoking protection and finding yourself in the clearing, then summoning your familiar. Explain that you want to discover your true self, to find out who you are. Ask to be taken to the place where your kind of being is most at home. You are asking to see the psychic equivalent of the plant's natural habitat. There are certain places where you are not at home, just as you wouldn't expect to see harebells in a jungle. And there *is* one kind of place where you are especially at home.

Your familiar will now lead you into the cave, down the usual passage and into the inner place of peace and beauty. After that, you may go anywhere at all. A door may open into the side of a hill. Within, you may find a whole country, some elven realm. Or a winged horse may take you to some other land, away across many seas and mountain ranges. You may travel to the past or to the future and you may even visit some remote planet. As in dreams, anything may now happen. And who is to say where your true spiritual home is? Perhaps on your own doorstep, some favoured sanctuary or place of pilgrimage. Perhaps not. Your familiar will guide you.

When you have reached the place, you must check out your familiar again, and ask, 'Is this my true home?' This must be done to make sure there has been no confusion. If there has, then you must move on again, until you are quite sure you have reached the right place.

Then look around you, wherever it is. And see what it is like there. What does this place suggest to you?

When you are ready, tell your familiar that you want to talk with the Spirit of the Place. This is a being, sometimes known as the *genius loci*, who is the place's essence. It will be a thought-form, an astral spirit, perhaps created by you, perhaps perceived as an already existing thought-form, created by others. It will be ensouled with the place's atmosphere, which is not created by you, but exists of itself. It may be a male or a female spirit, or may be androgynous. Your familiar will tell you where you should go for this, and how you may invoke him or her. Most probably you will only need to request aloud that the Spirit of the Place now appear before you. Do not forget to check that this being is genuine.

Greet the Spirit of the Place and explain why he or she has been called upon. Say that you understand that this is your true home, the place that gives rise to your type of being, and that you want to know your role within it, how you fit in. You want an answer to the question 'Who am I?' By now, you may already be beginning to have some idea, and thus may hear the answer spoken to you quite clearly. Or you may be shown some special item of clothing, or object, with clear association. For example, if the true nature of yourself were that of priestess, then you might be shown a robe you could associate with that role. Or if your true self were a traveller, some kind of explorer in mind or body, you might see a caravan or boat. Supposing you were truly some kind of seer, then you might see a crystal. A peacemaker? You might see doves. A scholar? Books may be held out towards you. There are endless possibilities. And the Spirit of the Place will explain to you the connection between the place and yourself.

You may be wondering why you need to ask who you are. Surely, in your essential self, you must be a witch? Perhaps. But it is equally possible that you are a healer, or guardian-of-Mother-Earth, but that you are called upon to play the role of witch, in this life. The self is constructed of many layers or facets. For example, a priestess may be called upon to play the role of witch in this incarnation. That may be what the Goddess wants of her, now. But in a former life, she may have been High Priestess in a temple of Isis. She may also have been a sybil at the Delphic oracle. She may even have been the woman who swept the floor in an Egyptian temple. But whatever the role, the common thread running through all her lives is that her nature is that of priestess. Of course, I have just used classic, even quite corny, examples. But the principle is the same, for priestess, scholar, healer or teacher. Whatever it is that you may be, the way in which you play it out changes, from life to life. I can almost hear you asking, 'What if I am really something quite ordinary? No healer, teacher or priestess, nothing elevated at all?' My answer is that no one is ordinary. We all have to do ordinary things, like housework, or play ordinary roles sometimes, like sister, schoolchild, employee, hospital patient, or 'member of the voting public.' But no one in a Goddess-orientated, non-hierarchical society would ever be regarded as some ordinary person, some 'nobody'. We are each and every one a hero or heroine on some kind of quest. And we each have some special kind of ability, whether it is healing, teaching, working magic, or nursing, tending plants, clowning or singing songs, or something else.

It is not our mundane tasks, but the quality that we bring to them, that shows the nature of the true self. And however oppressive the system under which we may be living in any particular incarnation, that self is constant and potentially creative, whoever we are.

When you have asked every question that you need to ask, in order to understand yourself, fully, you can request the Spirit of the Place to point out the plant which is your special emblem. For ever after, you will be able to call your true self, and your true home, to mind by visualizing this plant.

The knowledge of your self will have many implications. It may explain to you why you are at odds with your present life. Or it may tell you, instead, that though you had thought you were on the wrong path, you are actually not. Self-understanding will bring you to self-affirmation, and thus to a sense of your own worth. You will then be much stronger in pursuit of your true goals, being free of self-doubt (or as free as anyone open to change and discovery can ever be).

Ask the Spirit of the Place any further questions which you may now have. Then thank him or her. Retrace your route back to the lower cave, going by whatever means you came, for example the winged horse. Travel through the passageway to the usual upper cave, and then return to the clearing. Thank your familiar, return to the blue sphere, thank the Guardian Spirits and seal your aura.

Remember that the place you have just visited is your home, your true spiritual home. Wherever you go in the world, you can always return there. And you will always take some of its atmosphere and meaning with you, as emissary. If you have a need to recharge or reaffirm yourself, you can always go back there.

Of course, it could be argued that an emphasis on 'one true home' is not the best way to achieve a one-world (or one-universe) consciousness. I do not agree with this view. For it is not by denying our spiritual roots that we come to feel part of the All. The only real way to peace lies in accepting differences and then celebrating them, for diversity means life. (Mono-culture is no more to be recommended for souls than it is for plants.)

In the anonymity of modern society, a true awareness of one's essential self is beyond price. And that self can shine through the mundane tasks and the everyday roles, centring you and colouring your presence in all situations. This is the inner strength a witch needs, if she or he is to counsel or heal others, and work all kinds of magic, without feeling fragmented and off balance.

Blessed be,
Rae

Dear Tessa,

You have discovered by now that trance leads directly or indirectly to ritual, or to ritualized activity. Sometimes, a full formal rite is inspired by the guidance received – sometimes an informal rite, such as pilgrimage, or the wearing of certain clothes for symbolic reasons. And this, in turn, leads to transformation of a more far-reaching kind, to life changes. Trance and ritual are the two sides of magic, or, shall I say, the two tides: they flow back and forth into each other.

You ask why we need ritual, when so much can be accomplished in trance. I can only answer that a great deal is accomplished in dreams, and yet we must wake, must step out of the astral dream-world and act. Sleep and waking, the two sides of life. I suppose that trance is where the witch refreshes and restores her or himself, turning inwards to sources, to Goddess and God, that realm where her or his own spirit meets spirit in all things, to the inwardness, and to all sources. In ritual, the witch manifests this experience, he or she lives it out.

Trance is the gift of the Goddess, like all intuitive and psychic skills currently dismissed or half feared as 'women's intuition'. It is the business of witches and of all Goddess-worshippers to reclaim and to re-explain these lost skills, for they are one half of our understanding. They are the Moon's gift. The solar skills, rational thought-processes, the God's gift, are just as essential, if superstition is not to prevail. But logic on its own can become cold and machiavellian. (Look around at our logical and concrete world, and I do not think you will find that word too strong a description.) Logic on its own inverts, turning illogical; but the uniting of intuition and logic, true to the principles and aims of witchcraft, is a reconciliation of opposites, leading to life.

I am not trying to equate ritual with logic, for both trance and ritual are quite obviously transrational activities. But I am suggesting that there is passive (trance) and active (ritual) magic – the Goddess- and God-given realms of inner and outer life. If we grant that all magic really belongs to the Inner Realm, then trance is the inner and ritual the outer aspect of that.

I promised a letter about designing your own rites for specific purposes. This is a simple process, once you have grasped that all rites have the same component parts and that they slot into the same (or a similar) order each time.

The rite must be planned and then written out in your own Book of Shadows. This is the first step. Our ancestors would not have done this. Their minds were less cluttered than ours, and so the planned rite would have been memorized.

First, decide on the phase of Moon, or festival, according to your purpose. Which is the time most suited to your planned rite? If you are invoking for a new love, for example, then the Waxing or Full Moon days are the right choice.

Record the date on which you plan to work this rite, and then name it, for example: 'Ritual for the Invocation of Love and Happiness'.

Next, list the steps with which you begin every time. Thus: cast the circle; purify (by a short trance for psychic cleansing and balancing); invoke the Goddess and God. Every rite that you work should begin like this.

The fourth step is the statement of your intention, out loud. This is important, as it attunes your deep self to the coming work; and by it, you will become focused magically. It also tells all the Guardian Spirits, and your familiar, what you are meaning to achieve. You could say, for example:

Now the Moon waxes almost to the full. The time of fulfilment in love draws near. I, witch priestess and child of the Goddess work magic for love. I invoke love and happiness in my mind, spirit and soul and my body. So I call upon my rightful partner, and ask the blessings of the Goddess and God upon this, my rite of love and happiness.

Now you are ready for the fifth step, which is called 'the raising of magical energy'. You will probably do this by dancing (deosil in a love rite) and by chanting. The entry in your Book of Shadows (following your written statement of intention) should run something like this: *Dance deosil, to chant* —— (here you will write down the words of your planned chant).

The sixth step is called 'the directing of power'. It means that you now psychically direct the power that you have just raised into the main material focus of your planned spell.

This may be, for example, a small bowl of rose or rosewood oil, which you will have placed at the centre of your circle, inside your cauldron. Rose oil is sacred to love. (It is also extremely expensive! Nine drops diluted in a pure vegetable oil are sufficient.) Direct the power into the oil with your wand, or simply by cupping your hands over it. Visualize that the oil is now 'charged', imbued with the power you have raised, like a shining gold light.

The seventh step is called 'the work'. Whether celebratory or for a spell-casting, this is the peak of your rite. Now you will work magic. In the case of a love rite, you might now anoint your whole body with rose oil. You could then consecrate and anoint a small bell. And then speak your invocation. For example:

As he is wise, kind and beautiful,
let him now hear me.
As he is both gentle and sure of his own
purpose, his own direction,
as he is my true partner, strong to fulfil
and to be fulfilled by me,
now let him hear and come.
Let him hear and respond, knowing who calls.
And as his presence means happiness, and as I to him
am cup and wine, earth and flourishing tree, fruit-bearing,
so let him hear and come.

Ring the bell. Hear it reverberate in the astral realms. He

who answers your description will now hear it, for you have sent out your psychic call. It is important that conditions be laid down, as in the above spell: *As he is wise, kind and beautiful, etc. may he come.* This ensures that the spell won't work unless the prospective partner does have these qualities, and is therefore the right partner. But the words should be your own, and should be as simple or as elaborate as you want them. You may also spend some time in trance, both before and after the ringing of the bell.

You might next anoint a white or red cord with rose oil, saying:

> *As this knot is tied,*
> *so may the link be made,*
> *and may the link be love.*

(Of course, you can say words of your own choosing here. Mine are merely an example.) Then tie the two ends of the cord together, forming a circle.

The eighth step is called 'releasing'. Sit quietly in light trance, visualizing the effects of your bell-ringing and your tied knot. You may 'see' the sound of the bell note, as silver

motes dancing and travelling – and the cord as the completed circle, bringing into your life your true partner, making that link. See each spell leaving you and going out into the world to take effect. Let them go now. Let the outcome be in the hands of Goddess and God. So may it be.

The ninth step reaffirms you as child of the Goddess and God in the world, as one of all beings to whom you are one sister, both connected in and fulfilled by nature. This is called 'communion'. It, too, should be written into your Book of Shadows. It refers to the usual consecration of wine and bread, and the eating and drinking of these.

The tenth step is the thanking of the Goddess and God.

The eleventh step is the bidding of 'Hale and farewell' (with thanks) to all the Guardian Spirits. The circle is now opened. You step outside. The work is done.

To recap, these are the stages of any rite.

1. Cast the circle/define sacred space
2. Purify and centre
3. Invoke the Goddess and God
4. State magical intention
5. Raise the energy
6. Direct the energy
7. The work, magic, the spell-casting
8. Release the spell
9. Communion
10. Thanks to Goddess and God
11. Open circle and step outside

Let us say that you have been guided in trance about spells you must cast and rites you should work. Let us say you have then written out your planned rite, all the eleven steps of your rite. You will next need to buy or collect any herbs, oils, cords, stones, candles or whatever you must have. You will also want to select, gather or buy any flowers or whatever you want in your room, or upon your altar. That done, you are ready. When the chosen night comes, you must assemble all magical tools, have a bath and put on your robe. Be sure that you are free from interruption, then begin.

Afterwards, you should record experiences of this or any other rite. How did you feel? Was there clear guidance about the outcome? Any surprises? Was any material suggested for future trancework? Or is it all done? If you feel utterly at peace, complete, it is all done.

I hope these notes will be of help.

One last word of advice: never work spells that do not 'mix well' together. For example, a purification spell for the local environment, a banishing of ill-health for someone else, and an eradication of ill-luck for you, could all be done at the same (Waning Moon) rite. But do not mix a purification of the environment, a love spell which someone else has asked you to do, and a self-affirmation as witch and priestess. These would require different phases of the Moon, and they do not have common themes. It is the common themes which you should look for when choosing incense, altar flowers and the appropriate time. The same thing applies when you are planning a chant to raise power for more than one spell. If they are all about purification, in one way or another, sing about that. But if there is no common theme, you must separate them. Do more than one rite. In any case, it will always be easier to concentrate on just one spell, or one magical intention, as in the love rite. Experience is the best guide about blends and mixtures. And there is only one way to gain that....

Blessed be,
Rae

Dear Tessa,

This is the last letter I shall send for a while now. It is necessary that you put into practice some of these ideas in your own way. There is a tradition called 'voiding the coven' whereby a new High Priestess is cut off from almost all contact with the parent coven, until her own coven and her own style have become well established. We are not involved with covens, being solitary hedge witches, but I'm going to apply a similar principle to you, nonetheless. Of course, this does not mean that I do not want you to visit. I hope that you will be able to come the day after the summer solstice, as we have now provisionally arranged. I am looking forward to it very much. We can talk about the Craft and exchange news and ideas. But there will be no more lessons, for the time being.

Meanwhile, I want to write one last letter, about what I think it means to be a witch in everyday life. What are the pitfalls, the responsibilities and the pleasures? I have also enclosed a poem for you. It is my very personal view of what it means to be a witch. It is, I hope, a distilled essence, like all poems. This letter rambles on a bit more, and in more detail. Please read it first.

The first thing that I want to talk about is self-image: yours, as a witch. One problem with this is the thin line between hubris and humiliation. You will have to tread that line your whole life. On the side of hubris, arrogance, is the danger of thinking yourself all-powerful, or above mistakes. Your spells work! You are a witch then. Goddess and God and all the Guardian Spirits watch over you all the time. Therefore, of course, you are invulnerable, not like the ordinary men and women. I do not think that you would ever fall for this rubbish. But some people do. They start believing that they are beyond all human failing, all human doubts and fears. Our culture fosters this illusion, for the line goes something like this: 'If you are truly spiritual, truly in contact with the Gods and nature spirits, the realms of Ether, psychic and Inner Realms, then you do not have to worry about human problems. For your needs will be met if, that is, you are truly in contact. And if your needs are not all being met, then you can't be a real witch, or whatever you say you are.'

This is nonsense. No religion, no magical practice on Earth, ever can or even should take away all your human 'problems', your challenges and your creaturely bonds with all flesh and blood. Instead, magic is one kind of tool, and in some situations it is called for. And worship is the right and the fulfilment of all Earth's creatures, but not a universal panacea for all ills. Any witch knows that the loss of her or his magic would be impoverishment of the worst kind. To a witch, magic is life, just as music is life to a musician. Nevertheless, there is no magic in existence that can or should pre-empt the gift of your common humanity.

This brings me to the other side of that thin line, humiliation (the side I think that you could be likely to fall down on). People will sometimes imply or even directly say, 'What! A witch and yet you still have money worries/an unhappy love life/housing problems? Can't you really do spells then?'

You can tell them that magic, like ice-skating, does involve a certain amount of falling down on the job but that you are getting there! This is probably easier than explaining that your magical priorities are with, say, the environment and not your own purse. (They will silently accuse you of pretension if you say that.) It is also a lot easier than trying to explain that some spells fail because you are not wholeheartedly there when you cast them. Perhaps you are too angry, or too afraid of what the spell might demand in your everyday life. This kind of thing is about your own personal development and is really no one's business but your own.

People may also demand that you give your credentials as a 'white' witch by proving that you have no human faults. 'What! A witch priestess and yet you still shout at your children/fail to get on with your sister/often neglect to visit your ill and aged auntie? Thought you said it was a path that brought inner strength and peace.'

This kind of thing is best treated with humour. Because *of course* you are not perfect or you wouldn't be here on Earth, still learning. You can reply that you would have joined the Christian Church if you had had aspirations to saintliness. Meanwhile, you are doing your best to learn, to grow and to become integrated, and the path of the solitary witch is your chosen way. Humour combined with humility is the course recommended. It is better than trying to explain the truth to those who are not listening.

In fact, humility is a whole lot better than humiliation or hubris, any day. And it is probably the name of that thin line. I don't have to say all this. You already know it. But I suppose I am just trying to prepare you for the cruel questioners.

Your responsibility to witchcraft lies in fulfilling your role, in living as witch and priestess from day to day, in keeping the flame of nature magic burning and your own sense of wonder intact. It also lies in not bringing discredit upon your path. This does not mean, for example, that you should never have too much to drink at a party. You are not, as I have said, supposed to be inhuman. Real discredit lies in the misuse of your magic, or in the misuse of your role, to threaten or boast. Or in leaving a large and hypocritical gap between what you preach (respect for nature) and what you practise in your own life.

The pleasures of witchcraft you will already know about. And as the years go by, they deepen. They inform all your life, so that the magical resonance is felt in everything. From time to time, your pleasure in the psychic sensitivity a witch has will reach heights that afterwards you can never quite forget. You will have seen all the seasons as though they were newly created, and yet very ancient. As though from the first days. The essence of spring, summer, autumn and winter in flowers, warm landscapes, bright leaves and pure frost and snow. You will have seen the world of faerie, seen that *in the world*. Personally, I do not know how anyone who has ever seen such beauty could ever want anything as much as to enter that realm again. Not to possess it, but just to be there. That, I think, is what distinguishes the witch and Pagan. They have known that. Ever after, they work to bring that beauty out of Etheric realms – or perhaps to help this Earth to remove all the veils that humanity has put upon her.

The pleasures of witchcraft are quite easy to know, but not easy to write about.

I hope that you will enjoy the poem. It is called 'Resolution of a Witch' and is a kind of summer solstice present.

There is a task that I want you to do for me. Keep your own Book of Shadows well up to date for a whole year. Then answer me this question. 'What makes a Witch? As far as you are concerned, what makes a Witch?'

Myself, I think it is a kind of forest that the person has inside them. There are caves in it, wildflowers, and there are animals who are untamed. And there are birds, insects, grubs and worms, tangled roots, mosses, and also snakes. And there are streams, silver streams. Season follows season and there is wind in the trees, Sunlight, then darkness and starlight and the Moon. And there is always some kind of flame, like a candle flame inside a cave, and it shines everywhere that you go in that forest, shines out of the earth, and out of all the creatures. The witch has it too. It shines out of the forest within. It is called something like 'shadow-fire'. I can recognize it in another witch's eyes. I have seen it in yours.

Wise, merry and blessed be,
Rae

Resolution of a Witch

May I be as the one who weaves the cloth
in a forest, deep hidden.
May I sit at the work, uninterrupted.
And may I remain an outcast, if that is what it takes.
May I know the seasonal procession in my spirit and
in my body, celebrate cross quarters, solstices and equinoxes.
May each Full Moon find me looking upwards, at trees
outlined on luminous sky.
May I hold wildflowers. May I cup them in my hand.
May I then release them, unpicked,
to live on in abundance.
May my friends be of the kind who are at ease with silence.
May they and I be innocent of pretension.
May I be capable of gratitude. May I know
that I was given joy, like mother's milk.
May I know this as my dog does, in her bones and blood.
May I speak the truth about happiness and pain
in songs that sound of the scent of rosemary,
as everyday and ancient, kitchen-herb strong.
May I not incline to self-righteousness or self-pity.
May I approach the high earthworks and the stone circles
as fox or moth,
and disturb the place no more than that.
May my gaze be direct and my hand steady.
May my door be open to those who dwell outside wealth
and fame and privilege.
May those who have never walked barefoot never find the
   path
that leads up to my door.
May they be lost on the labyrinthine journey.

May they turn back.
And may I sit beside the fire in winter
and see in the glowing logs what is to come,
yet never feel the need to warn or to advise, unasked.
May I sit upon a plain wooden chair, in true contentment.
May the place where I live be as the forest.
May there be trackways where there are caves and pools
and trees and flowers, animals and birds,
all known to me and revered, loved.
May my existence change the world no more nor less
than the gusting of wind, or the proud growth of trees.
For this, I go in cast-off clothes.
May I keep faith, always.
May I never find excuses for the expedient.
May I know that I have no choice, and yet still make the
    choice
as the song is made, in joy, and with consideration.
May I make the same choice every day, again.
When I fail, may I know forgiveness for myself.
May I dance
naked, unafraid to face my own reflection.

By the same author

Reincarnation and the Dark Goddess
Lives and Teachings of a Priestess

Here are teachings about reincarnation from the viewpoint of a
present-day priestess. It is a look at the subject from the
balanced spiritual viewpoint of one who honours the Deep
Feminine, or Goddess, as Mother of Souls, as well as the Earth
Mother of physical existence.

In this light, and based on personal recollections, inner guidance and ancient teachings, the author explains individual
reincarnation as a microcosm of the Earth's great cycles of
existence and also as a means of developing human love and
wisdom in order to manifest the true beauty of the spirit realm.
Instructions are given for recall of past lives and the development of psychic skills. There are descriptions of the
Otherworld (where we go between lives) as the land of the
Dark Goddess – the Queen of the Dead. It is not a fearsome
place, but a joyful spirit land. Healing flows from within it,
whether we approach it or its peripheries in dreams, meditation
or between incarnations. The Dark Goddess is depicted as she
once was known – Mari, Kali, Tiamat, Isis, Persephone,
Morgaine, the Black Madonna – from cultures around the
world, and also as she can be understood now. Above all, this is
a rejoicing book. It describes psychic practices that promote
life and spirit healing, in the face of our repeated destructive-
ness of the Earth, and oppression of one another. This is a
sharing of a vision relevant to us all, in a process of discovery
and also rebirth.